A PARENT'S GUIDE TO ASCENT-BASED SUPPORT FOR AUTISM

PRACTICAL STRATEGIES, COMPASSIONATE TOOLS, AND ENCOURAGEMENT FOR HELPING YOUR CHILD THRIVE AND REACH THEIR FULL POTENTIAL

JENNIFER MELLER

First Edition: 2026

INTRODUCTION

Research from developmental psychologists reveals that up to eighty percent of parents raising children on the autism spectrum experience levels of daily stress comparable to active-duty combat veterans. This striking statistic is not meant to frighten you, but rather to validate the profound weight you carry every single day. This chronic exhaustion is not a personal failure, nor does it mean you lack patience. Instead, it is the natural consequence of navigating a societal landscape that frequently fails to understand your child's internal experience. When every transition, park visit, or family dinner feels like a high-stakes puzzle, your nervous system remains in a constant state of high alert.

Traditional parenting frameworks often reduce these complex neurodivergent experiences to a series of behaviors that must be modified, tracked, and corrected. This hyper-focus on outward compliance treats your child's reactions as isolated problems to solve rather than communication signals to decode. When we measure success solely by how well a child obeys a command or blends into a neurotypical environment, we overlook the immense internal effort they expend to feel safe. Children on the spectrum are not behaving badly; they are often simply trying to survive a sensory and emotional

environment that feels completely overwhelming. By shifting our focus from behavioral control to deep emotional safety, we build a foundation for genuine development.

Have you ever found yourself standing in a brightly lit grocery store aisle, watching your child experience an overwhelming meltdown, while strangers offer unhelpful whispers and silent judgment? In those moments, the instinct to demand compliance takes over, driven by anxiety and the desire for immediate peace. We try reward charts, strict boundaries, and behavioral prompts, only to find ourselves trapped in an exhausting cycle of temporary compliance followed by even greater behavioral regression. These superficial fixes do not Research from developmental psychologists reveals that up to eighty percent of parents raising children on the autism spectrum experience levels of daily stress comparable to active-duty combat veterans. This striking statistic is not meant to frighten you, but rather to validate the profound weight you carry every single day.

This chronic exhaustion is Research from developmental psychologists reveals that up to eighty percent of parents raising children on the autism spectrum experience levels of daily stress comparable to active-duty combat veterans. This striking statistic is not meant to frighten you, but rather to validate the profound weight you carry every single day. This chronic exhaustion is not a personal failure, nor does it mean you lack patience. Instead, it is the natural consequence of navigating a societal landscape that frequently fails to understand your child's internal experience. When every transition, park visit, or family dinner feels like a high-stakes puzzle, your nervous system remains in a constant state of high alert.

Traditional parenting frameworks often reduce these complex neurodivergent experiences to a series of behaviors that must be modified, tracked, and corrected. This hyper-focus on outward compliance treats your child's reactions as isolated problems to solve rather than communication signals to decode. When Research from developmental psychologists reveals that up to eighty percent of parents raising children on the autism spectrum experience levels of daily stress comparable to active-duty combat veterans. This striking statistic is not meant to frighten you, but rather to validate the profound weight you carry every single day. This chronic exhaustion is not a personal failure, nor does it mean you lack patience. Instead, it is the natural consequence of navigating a societal landscape that frequently fails to understand your child's internal experience. When every transition, park visit, or family dinner feels like a high-stakes puzzle, your nervous system remains in a constant state of high alert.

Traditional parenting frameworks often reduce these complex neurodivergent experiences to a series of behaviors that must be modified, tracked, and corrected. This hyper Research from developmental psychologists reveals that up to eighty percent of parents raising children on the autism spectrum experience levels of daily stress comparable to active-duty combat veterans. This striking statistic is not meant to frighten you, but rather to validate the profound weight you carry every single day. This chronic exhaustion is not a personal failure, nor does it mean you lack patience. Instead, it is the natural consequence of navigating a societal landscape that frequently fails to understand your child's internal experience. When every transition, park visit, or family dinner feels like a high-stakes puzzle, your nervous system remains in a constant state of high alert.

Traditional parenting frameworks often reduce these complex neurodivergent experiences to a series of behaviors that must be modified, tracked, and corrected. This hyper-focus on outward compliance treats your child's reactions as isolated problems to solve rather than communication signals to decode. When we measure success solely by how well a child obeys a command or blends into a neurotypical environment, we overlook the immense internal effort they expend to feel safe. Children on the spectrum are not behaving badly; they are often simply trying to survive a sensory and emotional environment that feels completely overwhelming. By shifting our focus from behavioral control to deep emotional safety, we build a foundation for genuine development.

Have you ever found yourself standing in a brightly lit grocery store aisle, watching your child experience an overwhelming meltdown, while strangers offer unhelpful whispers and silent judgment?

In those moments, the instinct to demand compliance takes over, driven by anxiety and the desire for immediate peace. We try reward charts, strict boundaries, and behavioral prompts, only to find ourselves trapped in an exhausting cycle of temporary compliance followed by even greater behavioral regression. These superficial fixes do not address the underlying neurological distress, leaving both you and your child feeling increasingly isolated. There is a far more sustainable way to navigate these challenges, one that does not require you to act as a behavioral warden.

The widely accepted clinical pursuit of compliance—getting a child to simply obey commands to fit neurotypical standards—frequently damages the very foundation of healthy development. When a child is repeatedly forced to mask their sensory discomfort or emotional dysregulation, they learn to suppress their authentic self, leading to intense internal anxiety and eventual burnout. Real development does not occur through forced compliance; it flourishes through natural developmental progress built on a foundation of safety. When we prioritize compliance over connection, we inadvertently teach our children that their internal experiences are invalid, eroding the mutual trust that is vital for long-term growth. True progress begins when we stop asking how to change our child's behavior and start asking how we can support their nervous system.

Every single day, well-meaning parents wake up exhausted, immediately bracing themselves for an invisible battle against sudden transitions, sensory overloads, and unpredictable meltdowns. You might spend your evenings scrolling through endless online forums, searching for a magical routine or a therapeutic breakthrough that will finally bring peace to your living room. The sheer volume of conflicting advice can leave you feeling paralyzed, second-guessing your maternal or paternal instincts at every turn. It feels as though you are constantly walking on eggshells, waiting for the next sensory trigger to disrupt the fragile harmony of your home. This chronic state of worry deprives you of the simple, joyful moments of parenthood that you so richly deserve.

You might be secretly harboring a deep, heavy sense of guilt, constantly wondering if you did something wrong or if you are failing to provide the right environment for your child to thrive. This guilt is often compounded by well-meaning relatives, educators, and doctors who imply that firmer discipline would solve your child's behavioral challenges. It is easy to fall into the trap of comparing your family's daily life to the seemingly effortless routines of neurotypical families in your neighborhood. Please understand that your child's developmental differences are not a reflection of poor parenting, and your feelings of frustration do not make you a bad parent. You are navigating a complex neurological journey without an adequate map, and it is completely natural to feel overwhelmed.

Deep down, you do not Research from developmental psychologists reveals that up to eighty percent of parents raising children on the autism spectrum experience levels of daily stress comparable to active-duty combat veterans. This striking statistic is not meant to frighten you, but rather to validate the profound weight you carry every single day. This chronic exhaustion is not a personal failure, nor does it mean you lack patience. Instead, it is the natural consequence of navigating a societal landscape that frequently fails to understand your child's internal experience. When every transition, park visit, or family dinner feels like a high-stakes puzzle, your nervous system remains in a constant state of high alert.

Traditional parenting frameworks often reduce these complex neurodivergent experiences to a series of behaviors that must be modified, tracked, and corrected. This hyper-focus on outward compliance treats your child's reactions as isolated problems to solve rather than communication signals to decode. When we measure success solely by how well a child obeys a command or blends into a neurotypical environment, we overlook the immense internal effort they expend to feel safe. Children on the spectrum are not behaving badly; they are often simply trying to survive a sensory and emotional environment that feels completely overwhelming. By shifting our focus from behavioral control to deep emotional safety, we build a foundation for genuine development.

Have you ever found yourself standing in a brightly lit grocery store aisle, watching your child Research from developmental psychologists reveals that up to eighty percent of parents raising children on the autism spectrum experience levels of daily stress comparable to active-duty combat veterans. This striking statistic is not meant to frighten you, but rather to validate the profound weight you carry every single day. This chronic exhaustion is not a personal failure, nor does it mean you lack patience. Instead, it is the natural consequence of navigating a societal landscape that frequently fails to understand your child's internal experience. When every transition, park visit, or family dinner feels like a high-stakes puzzle, your nervous system remains in a constant state of high alert.

Traditional parenting frameworks often reduce these complex neurodivergent experiences to a series of behaviors that must be modified, tracked, and corrected. This hyper-focus on outward compliance treats your child's reactions as isolated problems to solve rather than communication signals to decode. When we measure success solely by how well a child obeys a command or blends into a neurotypical environment, we overlook the immense internal effort they expend to feel safe. Children on the spectrum are not behaving badly; they are often simply trying to survive a sensory and emotional environment that feels completely overwhelming. By shifting our focus from behavioral control to deep emotional safety, we build a foundation for genuine development.

Have you ever found yourself standing in a brightly lit grocery store aisle, watching your child experience an overwhelming meltdown, while strangers offer unhelpful whispers and silent judgment? In those moments, the instinct to demand compliance Research from developmental psychologists reveals that up to eighty percent of parents raising children on the autism spectrum experience levels of daily stress comparable to active-duty combat veterans. This striking statistic is not meant to frighten you, but rather to validate the profound weight you carry every single day. This chronic exhaustion is not a personal failure, nor does it mean you lack patience. Instead, it is the natural consequence of navigating a societal landscape that frequently fails to understand your child's internal experience. When every transition, park visit, or family dinner feels like a high-stakes puzzle, your nervous system remains in a constant state of high alert.

Traditional parenting frameworks often reduce these complex neurodivergent experiences to a series of behaviors that must be modified, tracked, and corrected. This hyper-focus on outward compliance treats your child's reactions as isolated problems to solve rather than communication signals to decode. When we measure success solely by how well a child obeys a command or blends into a neurotypical environment, we overlook the immense internal effort they expend to feel safe. Children on the spectrum are not behaving badly; they are often simply trying to survive a sensory and emotional environment that feels completely overwhelming. By shifting our focus from behavioral control to deep emotional safety, we build a foundation for genuine development.

Have you ever found yourself standing in a brightly lit grocery store aisle, watching your child experience an overwhelming meltdown, while strangers offer unhelpful whispers and silent judgment? In those moments, the instinct to demand compliance takes over, driven by anxiety and the desire for immediate peace. We try reward charts, strict boundaries, and behavioral prompts, only to find ourselves trapped in an exhausting cycle of temporary compliance followed by even greater behavioral regression. These superficial fixes do not address the underlying neurological distress, leaving both you and your child feeling increasingly isolated. There is a far more sustainable way to navigate these challenges, one that does not require you to act as a behavioral warden.

The widely accepted clinical pursuit of compliance—getting a child to simply obey commands to fit neurotypical standards—frequently damages the very foundation of healthy development. When a child is repeatedly forced to mask their sensory discomfort or emotional dysregulation, they learn to suppress their authentic self, leading to intense internal anxiety and eventual burnout. Real development does not occur through forced compliance; it flourishes through natural developmental progress built on a foundation of safety. When we prioritize compliance over connection, we inadvertently teach our children that Research from developmental psychologists reveals that up to eighty percent of parents raising children on the autism spectrum experience levels of daily stress comparable to active-duty combat veterans. This striking statistic is not meant to frighten you, but rather to validate the profound weight you carry every single day. This chronic exhaustion is not a personal failure, nor does it mean you lack patience. Instead, it is the natural consequence of navigating a societal landscape that frequently fails to understand your child's internal experience. When every transition, park visit, or family dinner feels like a high-stakes puzzle, your nervous system remains in a constant state of high alert.

Traditional parenting frameworks often reduce these complex neurodivergent experiences to a series of behaviors that must be modified, tracked, and corrected. This hyper-focus on outward compliance treats your child's reactions as isolated problems to solve rather than communication signals to decode. When we measure success solely by how well a child obeys a command or blends into a neurotypical environment, we overlook the immense internal effort they expend to feel safe. Children on the spectrum are not behaving badly; they are often simply trying to survive a sensory and emotional environment that feels completely overwhelming. By shifting our focus from behavioral control to deep emotional safety, we build a foundation for genuine development.

Have you ever found yourself standing in a brightly lit grocery store aisle, watching your child experience an overwhelming meltdown, while strangers offer unhelpful whispers and silent judgment? In those moments, the instinct to demand compliance takes over, driven by anxiety and the desire for immediate peace. We try reward charts, strict boundaries, and behavioral prompts, only to find ourselves trapped in an exhausting cycle of temporary compliance followed by even greater behavioral regression. These superficial fixes do not address the underlying neurological distress, leaving both you and your child feeling increasingly isolated. There is a far more sustainable way to navigate these challenges, one that does not require you to act as a behavioral warden.

The widely accepted clinical pursuit of compliance—getting a child to simply obey commands to fit neurotypical standards—frequently damages the very foundation of healthy development. When a child is repeatedly forced to mask their sensory discomfort or emotional dysregulation, they learn to suppress their authentic self Research from developmental psychologists reveals that up to eighty percent of parents raising children on the autism spectrum experience levels of daily stress comparable to active-duty combat veterans. This striking statistic is not meant to frighten you, but rather to validate the profound weight you carry every single day. This chronic exhaustion is not a personal failure, nor does it mean you lack patience. Instead, it is the natural consequence of navigating a societal landscape that frequently fails to understand your child's internal experience. When every transition, park visit, or family dinner feels like a high-stakes puzzle, your nervous system remains in a constant state of high alert.

Traditional parenting frameworks often reduce these complex neurodivergent experiences to a series of behaviors that must be modified, tracked, and corrected. This hyper-focus on outward compliance treats your child's reactions as isolated problems to solve rather than communication signals to decode. When we measure success solely by how well a child obeys a command or blends into a neurotypical environment, we overlook the immense internal effort they expend to feel safe. Children on the spectrum are not behaving badly; they are often simply trying to survive a sensory and emotional environment that feels completely overwhelming. By shifting our focus from behavioral control to deep emotional safety, we build a foundation for genuine development.

Have you ever found yourself standing in a brightly lit grocery store aisle, watching your child experience an overwhelming meltdown, while strangers offer unhelpful whispers and silent judgment? In those moments, the instinct to demand compliance takes over, driven by anxiety and the desire for immediate peace. We try reward charts, strict boundaries, and behavioral prompts, only to find ourselves trapped in an exhausting cycle of temporary compliance followed by even greater behavioral regression. These superficial fixes do not address the underlying neurological distress, leaving both you and your child feeling increasingly isolated. There is a far more sustainable way to navigate these challenges, one that does not require you to act as a behavioral warden.

The widely accepted clinical pursuit of compliance—getting a child to simply obey commands to fit neurotypical standards—frequently damages the very foundation of healthy development. When a child is repeatedly forced to mask their sensory discomfort or emotional dysregulation, they learn to suppress their authentic self, leading to intense internal anxiety and eventual burnout. Real development does not occur through forced compliance; it flourishes through Research from developmental psychologists reveals that up to eighty percent of parents raising children on the autism spectrum experience levels of daily stress comparable to active-duty combat veterans. This striking statistic is not meant to frighten you, but rather to validate the profound weight you carry every single day. This chronic exhaustion is not a personal failure, nor does it mean you lack patience. Instead, it is the natural consequence of navigating a societal landscape that frequently fails to understand your child's internal experience. When every transition, park visit, or family dinner feels like a high-stakes puzzle, your nervous system remains in a constant state of high alert.

Traditional parenting frameworks often reduce these complex neurodivergent experiences to a series of behaviors that must be modified, tracked, and corrected. This hyper-focus on outward compliance treats your child's reactions as isolated problems to solve rather than communication signals to decode. When we measure success solely by how well a child obeys a command or blends into a neurotypical environment, we overlook the immense internal effort they expend to feel safe. Children on the spectrum are not behaving badly; they are often simply trying to survive a sensory and emotional environment that feels completely overwhelming. By shifting our focus from behavioral control to deep emotional safety, we build a foundation for genuine development.

Have you ever found yourself standing in a brightly lit grocery store aisle, watching your child experience an overwhelming meltdown, while strangers offer unhelpful whispers and silent judgment? In those moments, the instinct to demand compliance takes over, driven by anxiety and the desire for immediate peace. We try reward charts, strict boundaries, and behavioral prompts, only to find ourselves trapped in an exhausting cycle of temporary compliance followed by even greater behavioral regression. These superficial fixes do not address the underlying neurological distress, leaving both you and your child feeling increasingly isolated. There is a far more sustainable way to navigate these challenges, one that does not require you to act as a behavioral warden.

The widely accepted clinical pursuit of compliance—getting a child to simply obey commands to fit neurotypical standards—frequently damages the very foundation of healthy development. When a child is repeatedly forced to mask their sensory discomfort or emotional dysregulation, they learn to suppress their authentic self, leading to intense internal anxiety and eventual burnout. Real development does not occur through forced compliance; it flourishes through natural developmental progress built on a foundation of safety. When we prioritize compliance over connection, we inadvertently teach our children that their internal experiences are invalid, eroding the mutual trust that is vital for long-term growth. True progress begins when we stop asking how to change our child's behavior and start asking how we can support their nervous system.

Every single day, well-meaning parents wake up exhausted, immediately bracing themselves for an invisible battle against sudden transitions, sensory overloads, and unpredictable meltdowns. You might spend your evenings scrolling through endless online forums, searching for a magical routine or a therapeutic breakthrough that will finally bring peace to your living room. The sheer volume of conflicting advice can leave you feeling paralyzed, second-guessing your maternal or paternal instincts at every turn. It feels as though you are constantly walking on eggshells Research from developmental psychologists reveals that up to eighty percent of parents raising children on the autism spectrum experience levels of daily stress comparable to active-duty combat veterans. This striking statistic is not meant to frighten you, but rather to validate the profound weight you carry every single day. This chronic exhaustion is not a personal failure, nor does it mean you lack patience. Instead, it is the natural consequence of navigating a societal landscape that frequently fails to understand your child's internal experience. When every transition, park visit, or family dinner feels like a high-stakes puzzle, your nervous system remains in a constant state of high alert.

Traditional parenting frameworks often reduce these complex neurodivergent experiences to a series of behaviors that must be modified, tracked, and corrected. This hyper-focus on outward compliance treats your child's reactions as isolated problems to solve rather than communication signals to decode. When we measure success solely by how well a child obeys a command or blends into a neurotypical environment, we overlook the immense internal effort they expend to feel safe. Children on the spectrum are not behaving badly; they are often simply trying to survive a sensory and emotional environment that feels completely overwhelming. By shifting our focus from behavioral control to deep emotional safety, we build a foundation for genuine development.

Have you ever found yourself standing in a brightly lit grocery store aisle, watching your child experience an overwhelming meltdown, while strangers offer unhelpful whispers and silent judgment? In those moments, the instinct to demand compliance takes over, driven by anxiety and the desire for immediate peace. We try reward charts, strict boundaries, and behavioral prompts, only to find ourselves trapped in an exhausting cycle of temporary compliance followed by even greater behavioral regression. These superficial fixes do not address the underlying neurological distress, leaving both you and your child feeling increasingly isolated. There is a far more sustainable way to navigate these challenges, one that does not require you to act as a behavioral warden.

The widely accepted clinical pursuit of compliance—getting a child to simply obey commands to fit neurotypical standards—

frequently damages the very foundation of healthy development. When a child is repeatedly forced to mask their sensory discomfort or emotional dysregulation, they learn to suppress their authentic self, leading to intense internal anxiety and eventual burnout. Real development does not occur through forced compliance; it flourishes through natural developmental progress built on a foundation of safety. When we prioritize compliance over connection, we inadvertently teach our children that their internal experiences are invalid, eroding the mutual trust that is vital for long-term growth. True progress begins when we stop asking how to change our child's behavior and start asking how we can support their nervous system.

Every single day, well-meaning parents wake up exhausted, immediately bracing themselves for an invisible battle against sudden transitions, sensory overloads, and unpredictable meltdowns. You might spend your evenings scrolling through endless online forums, searching for a magical routine or Research from developmental psychologists reveals that up to eighty percent of parents raising children on the autism spectrum experience levels of daily stress comparable to active-duty combat veterans. This striking statistic is not meant to frighten you, but rather to validate the profound weight you carry every single day. This chronic exhaustion is not a personal failure, nor does it mean you lack patience. Instead, it is the natural consequence of navigating a societal landscape that frequently fails to understand your child's internal experience. When every transition, park visit, or family dinner feels like a high-stakes puzzle, your nervous system remains in a constant state of high alert.

Traditional parenting frameworks often reduce these complex neurodivergent experiences to a series of behaviors that must be modified, tracked, and corrected. This hyper-focus on outward compliance treats your child's reactions as isolated problems to solve rather than communication signals to decode. When we measure success solely by how well a child obeys a command or blends into a neurotypical environment, we overlook the immense internal effort they expend to feel safe. Children on the spectrum are not behaving badly; they are often simply trying to survive a sensory and emotional

environment that feels completely overwhelming. By shifting our focus from behavioral control to deep emotional safety, we build a foundation for genuine development.

Have you ever found yourself standing in a brightly lit grocery store aisle, watching your child experience an overwhelming meltdown, while strangers offer unhelpful whispers and silent judgment? In those moments, the instinct to demand compliance takes over, driven by anxiety and the desire for immediate peace. We try reward charts, strict boundaries, and behavioral prompts, only to find ourselves trapped in an exhausting cycle of temporary compliance followed by even greater behavioral regression. These superficial fixes do not address the underlying neurological distress, leaving both you and your child feeling increasingly isolated. There is a far more sustainable way to navigate these challenges, one that does not require you to act as a behavioral warden.

The widely accepted clinical pursuit of compliance—getting a child to simply obey commands to fit neurotypical standards—frequently damages the very foundation of healthy development. When a child is repeatedly forced to mask their sensory discomfort or emotional dysregulation, they learn to suppress their authentic self, leading to intense internal anxiety and eventual burnout. Real development does not occur through forced compliance; it flourishes through natural developmental progress built on a foundation of safety. When we prioritize compliance over connection, we inadvertently teach our children that their internal experiences are invalid, eroding the mutual trust that is vital for long-term growth. True progress begins when we stop asking how to change our child's behavior and start asking how we can support their nervous system.

Every single day, well-meaning parents wake up exhausted, immediately bracing themselves for an invisible battle against sudden transitions, sensory overloads, and unpredictable meltdowns. You might spend your evenings scrolling through endless online forums, searching for a magical routine or a therapeutic breakthrough that will finally bring peace to your living room. The sheer volume of conflicting advice can leave you feeling paralyzed, second-guessing your maternal or paternal instincts at every turn. It feels as though you are constantly walking on eggshells, waiting for the next sensory trigger to disrupt the fragile harmony of your home. This chronic state of worry deprives you of the simple, joyful moments of parenthood that you so richly deserve.

You might be secretly harboring a deep, heavy sense of guilt, constantly wondering if you did something wrong or if you are failing to provide the right environment for your child to thrive. This guilt is often compounded by well-meaning relatives, educators, and doctors who imply that firmer discipline would solve your child's behavioral challenges. It is easy to fall into the trap of comparing your family's daily life to the seemingly effortless routines of neurotypical families in your neighborhood. Please understand that your child's developmental differences are not a reflection of poor parenting, and your feelings of frustration do not make you a bad parent.

You are navigating a Research from developmental psychologists reveals that up to eighty percent of parents raising children on the autism spectrum experience levels of daily stress comparable to active-duty combat veterans. This striking statistic is not meant to frighten you, but rather to validate the profound weight you carry every single day. This chronic exhaustion is not a personal failure, nor does it mean you lack patience. Instead, it is the natural consequence of navigating a societal landscape that frequently fails to understand your child's internal experience. When every transition, park visit, or family dinner feels like a high-stakes puzzle, your nervous system remains in a constant state of high alert.

Traditional parenting frameworks often reduce these complex neurodivergent experiences to a series of behaviors that must be modified, tracked, and corrected. This hyper-focus on outward compliance treats your child's reactions as isolated problems to solve rather than communication signals to decode. When we measure success solely by how well a child obeys a command or blends into a neurotypical environment, we overlook the immense internal effort they expend to feel safe. Children on the spectrum are not behaving badly; they are often simply trying to survive a sensory and emotional

environment that feels completely overwhelming. By shifting our focus from behavioral control to deep emotional safety, we build a foundation for genuine development.

Have you ever found yourself standing in a brightly lit grocery store aisle, watching your child experience an overwhelming meltdown, while strangers offer unhelpful whispers and silent judgment? In those moments, the instinct to demand compliance takes over, driven by anxiety and the desire for immediate peace. We try reward charts, strict boundaries, and behavioral prompts, only to find ourselves trapped in an exhausting cycle of temporary compliance followed by even greater behavioral regression. These superficial fixes do not address the underlying neurological distress, leaving both you and your child feeling increasingly isolated. There is a far more sustainable way to navigate these challenges, one that does not require you to act as a behavioral warden.

The widely accepted clinical pursuit of compliance—getting a child to simply obey commands to fit neurotypical standards—frequently damages the very foundation of healthy development. When a child is repeatedly forced to mask their sensory discomfort or emotional dysregulation, they learn to suppress their authentic self, leading to intense internal anxiety and eventual burnout. Real development does not occur through forced compliance; it flourishes through natural developmental progress built on a foundation of safety. When we prioritize compliance over connection, we inadvertently teach our children that their internal experiences are invalid, eroding the mutual trust that is vital for long-term growth. True progress begins when we stop asking how to change our child's behavior and start asking how we can support their nervous system.

Every single day, well-meaning parents wake up exhausted, immediately bracing themselves for an invisible battle against sudden transitions, sensory overloads, and unpredictable meltdowns. You might spend your evenings scrolling through endless online forums, searching for a magical routine or a therapeutic breakthrough that will finally bring peace to your living room. The sheer volume of conflicting advice can leave you feeling paralyzed, second-guessing your maternal or paternal instincts at every turn. It feels as though you are constantly walking on eggshells, waiting for the next sensory trigger to disrupt the fragile harmony of your home. This chronic state of worry deprives you of the simple, joyful moments of parenthood that you so richly deserve.

You might be secretly harboring a deep, heavy sense of guilt, constantly wondering if you did something wrong or if you are failing to provide the right environment for your Research from developmental psychologists reveals that up to eighty percent of parents raising children on the autism spectrum experience levels of daily stress comparable to active-duty combat veterans. This striking statistic is not meant to frighten you, but rather to validate the profound weight you carry every single day. This chronic exhaustion is not a personal failure, nor does it mean you lack patience. Instead, it is the natural consequence of navigating a societal landscape that frequently fails to understand your child's internal experience. When every transition, park visit, or family dinner feels like a high-stakes puzzle, your nervous system remains in a constant state of high alert.

Traditional parenting frameworks often reduce these complex neurodivergent experiences to a series of behaviors that must be modified, tracked, and corrected. This hyper-focus on outward compliance treats your child's reactions as isolated problems to solve rather than communication signals to decode. When we measure success solely by how well a child obeys a command or blends into a neurotypical environment, we overlook the immense internal effort they expend to feel safe. Children on the spectrum are not behaving badly; they are often simply trying to survive a sensory and emotional environment that feels completely overwhelming. By shifting our focus from behavioral control to deep emotional safety, we build a foundation for genuine development.

Have you ever found yourself standing in a brightly lit grocery store aisle, watching your child experience an overwhelming meltdown, while strangers offer unhelpful whispers and silent judgment? In those moments, the instinct to demand compliance takes over, driven by anxiety and the desire for immediate peace. We try reward charts, strict boundaries, and behavioral prompts, only to find ourselves trapped in an exhausting cycle of temporary compliance followed by even greater behavioral regression. These superficial fixes do not address the underlying neurological distress, leaving both you and your child feeling increasingly isolated. There is a far more sustainable way to navigate these challenges, one that does not require you to act as a behavioral warden.

The widely accepted clinical pursuit of compliance—getting a child to simply obey commands to fit neurotypical standards—frequently damages the very foundation of healthy development. When a child is repeatedly forced to mask their sensory discomfort or emotional dysregulation, they learn to suppress their authentic self, leading to intense internal anxiety and eventual burnout. Real development does not occur through forced compliance; it flourishes through natural developmental progress built on a foundation of safety. When we prioritize compliance over connection, we inadvertently teach our children that their internal experiences are invalid, eroding the mutual trust that is vital for long-term growth. True progress begins when we stop asking how to change our child's behavior and start asking how we can support their nervous system.

Every single day, well-meaning parents wake up exhausted, immediately bracing themselves for an invisible battle against sudden transitions, sensory overloads, and unpredictable meltdowns. You might spend your evenings scrolling through endless online forums, searching for a magical routine or a therapeutic breakthrough that will finally bring peace to your living room. The sheer volume of conflicting advice can leave you feeling paralyzed, second-guessing your maternal or paternal instincts at every turn. It feels as though you are constantly walking on eggshells, waiting for the next sensory trigger to disrupt the fragile harmony of your home. This chronic state of worry deprives you of the simple, joyful moments of parenthood that you so richly deserve.

You might be secretly harboring a deep, heavy sense of guilt, constantly wondering if you did something wrong or if you are failing to provide the right environment for your child to thrive. This guilt is often compounded by well-meaning relatives, educators, and doctors who imply that firmer discipline would solve your child's behavioral challenges. It is easy to fall into the trap of comparing your family's daily life to the seemingly effortless routines of neurotypical families in your neighborhood. Please understand that your child's developmental differences are not a reflection of poor parenting, and your feelings of frustration do not make you a bad parent. You are navigating a complex neurological journey without an adequate map, and it is completely natural to feel overwhelmed.

Deep down, you do not want a compliance-driven household where your child simply follows orders out of fear; you want a home of genuine connection and understanding. You long for those beautiful, quiet moments of shared joy, where your child looks at you with absolute trust, feeling completely safe in their own skin. You desire a practical daily routine that supports your child's unique developmental pacing while reducing the frequency and severity of exhausting meltdowns. Ultimately, your goal is to help your child develop genuine independence, social confidence, and emotional resilience so they can successfully navigate the world on their own terms. This book is designed to show you that this hopeful future is entirely within your reach.

A beautiful shift occurs when we stop trying to fix behavioral symptoms Research from developmental psychologists reveals that up to eighty percent of parents raising children on the autism spectrum experience levels of daily stress comparable to active-duty combat veterans. This striking statistic is not meant to frighten you, but rather to validate the profound weight you carry every single day. This chronic exhaustion is not a personal failure, nor does it mean you lack patience. Instead, it is the natural consequence of navigating a societal landscape that frequently fails to understand your child's internal experience. When every transition, park visit, or family dinner feels like a high-stakes puzzle, your nervous system remains in a constant state of high alert.

Traditional parenting frameworks often reduce these complex neurodivergent experiences to a series of behaviors that must be modified, tracked, and corrected. This hyper-focus on outward compliance treats your child's reactions as isolated problems to solve rather than communication signals to decode. When we measure success solely by how well a child obeys a command or blends into a neurotypical environment, we overlook the immense internal effort they expend to feel safe. Children on the spectrum are not behaving badly; they are often simply trying to survive a sensory and emotional environment that feels completely overwhelming. By shifting our focus from behavioral control to deep emotional safety, we build a foundation for genuine development.

Have you ever found yourself standing in a brightly lit grocery store aisle, watching your child experience an overwhelming meltdown, while strangers offer unhelpful whispers and silent judgment? In those moments, the instinct to demand compliance takes over, driven by anxiety and the desire for immediate peace. We try reward charts, strict boundaries, and behavioral prompts, only to find ourselves trapped in an exhausting cycle of temporary compliance followed by even greater behavioral regression. These superficial fixes do not address the underlying neurological distress, leaving both you and your child feeling increasingly isolated. There is a far more sustainable way to navigate these challenges, one that does not require you to act as a behavioral warden.

The widely accepted clinical pursuit of compliance—getting a child to simply obey commands to fit neurotypical standards—frequently damages the very foundation of healthy development. When a child is repeatedly forced to mask their sensory discomfort or emotional dysregulation, they learn to suppress their authentic self, leading to intense internal anxiety and eventual burnout. Real development does not occur through forced compliance; it flourishes through natural developmental progress built on a foundation of safety. When we prioritize compliance over connection, we inadvertently teach our children that their internal experiences are invalid, eroding the mutual trust that is vital for long-term growth. True progress begins when we stop asking how to change our child's behavior and start asking how we can support their nervous system.

Every single day, well-meaning parents wake up exhausted, immediately bracing themselves for an invisible battle against sudden transitions, sensory overloads, and unpredictable meltdowns. You might spend your evenings scrolling through endless online forums, searching for a magical routine or a therapeutic breakthrough that will finally bring peace to your living room. The sheer volume of conflicting advice can leave you feeling paralyzed, second-guessing your maternal or paternal instincts at every turn. It feels as though you are constantly walking on eggshells, waiting for the next sensory trigger to disrupt the fragile harmony of your home. This chronic state of worry deprives you of the simple, joyful moments of parenthood that you so richly deserve.

You might be secretly harboring a deep, heavy sense of guilt, constantly wondering if you did something wrong or if you are failing to provide the right environment for your child to thrive. This guilt is often compounded by well-meaning relatives, educators, and doctors who imply that firmer discipline would solve your child's behavioral challenges. It is easy to fall into the trap of comparing your family's daily life to the seemingly effortless routines of neurotypical families in your neighborhood. Please understand that your child's developmental differences are not a reflection of poor parenting, and your feelings of frustration do not make you a bad parent. You are navigating a complex neurological journey without an adequate map, and it is completely natural to feel overwhelmed.

Deep down, you do not want a compliance-driven household where your child simply follows orders out of fear; you want a home of genuine connection and understanding. You long for those beautiful, quiet moments of shared joy, where your child looks at you with absolute trust, feeling completely safe in their own skin. You desire a practical daily routine that supports your child's unique developmental pacing while reducing the frequency and severity of exhausting meltdowns. Ultimately, your goal is to help your child develop genuine independence, social confidence, and emotional resilience so they can successfully navigate the world on their own terms. This book is designed to show you that this hopeful future is entirely within your reach.

A beautiful shift occurs when we stop trying to fix behavioral symptoms and start addressing the sensory and emotional needs driving them. By embracing a connection-first framework, you can cultivate a home environment where meltdowns naturally decrease because your child feels deeply understood and neurologically safe. You will move away from the exhausting role of a constant behavior-tracker and step into the role of an intuitive, supportive guide. This approach does not require you to tolerate destructive behavior, but rather empowers you to understand the *sensory and emotional why Research from developmental psychologists reveals that up to eighty percent of parents raising children on the autism spectrum experience levels of daily stress comparable to active-duty combat veterans. This striking statistic is not meant to frighten you, but rather to validate the profound weight you carry every single day. This chronic exhaustion is not a personal failure, nor does it mean you lack patience. Instead, it is the natural consequence of navigating a societal landscape that frequently fails to understand your child's internal experience. When every transition, park visit, or family dinner feels like a high-stakes puzzle, your nervous system remains in a constant state of high alert.*

Traditional parenting frameworks often reduce these complex neurodivergent experiences to a series of behaviors that must be modified, tracked, and corrected. This hyper-focus on outward compliance treats your child's reactions as isolated problems to solve rather than communication signals to decode. When we measure success solely by how well a child obeys a command or blends into a neurotypical environment, we overlook the immense internal effort they expend to feel safe. Children on the spectrum are not behaving badly; they are often simply trying to survive a sensory and emotional environment that feels completely overwhelming. By shifting our focus from behavioral control to deep emotional safety, we build a foundation for genuine development. Have you ever found yourself standing in a brightly lit grocery store aisle, watching your child experience an overwhelming meltdown, while strangers offer unhelpful whispers and silent judgment? In those moments, the instinct to demand compliance takes over, driven by anxiety and the desire for immediate peace. We try reward charts, strict boundaries, and behavioral prompts, only to find ourselves trapped in an exhausting cycle of temporary compliance followed by even greater behavioral regression. These superficial fixes do not address the underlying neurological distress, leaving both you and your child feeling increasingly isolated. There is a far more sustainable way to navigate these challenges, one that does not require you to act as a behavioral warden. The widely accepted clinical pursuit of compliance—getting a child to simply obey commands to fit neurotypical standards—frequently damages the very foundation of healthy development. When a child is repeatedly forced to mask their sensory discomfort or emotional dysregulation, they learn to suppress their authentic self, leading to intense internal anxiety and eventual burnout. Real development does not occur through forced compliance; it flourishes through natural developmental progress built on a foundation of safety. When we prioritize compliance over connection, we inadvertently teach our children that their internal experiences are invalid, eroding the mutual trust that is vital for long-term growth. True progress begins when we stop asking how to change our child's behavior and start asking how we can support their nervous system. Every single day, well-meaning parents wake up exhausted, immediately bracing themselves for an invisible battle against sudden transitions, sensory overloads, and unpredictable meltdowns. You might spend your evenings scrolling through endless online forums, searching for a magical routine or a therapeutic breakthrough that will finally bring peace to your living room. The sheer volume of conflicting advice can leave you feeling paralyzed, second-guessing your maternal or paternal instincts at every turn. It feels as though you are constantly walking on eggshells, waiting for the next sensory trigger to disrupt the fragile harmony of your home. This chronic state of worry deprives you of the simple, joyful moments of parenthood that you so richly deserve. You might be secretly harboring a deep, heavy sense of guilt, constantly wondering if you did something wrong or if you are failing to provide the right environment for your child to thrive. This guilt is often compounded by well-meaning relatives, educators, and doctors who imply that firmer discipline would solve your child's behavioral challenges. It is easy to fall into the trap of comparing your family's daily life to the seemingly effortless routines of neurotypical families in your neighborhood. Please understand that your child's developmental differences are not a reflection of poor parenting, and your feelings of frustration do not make you a bad parent. You are navigating a complex neurological journey without an adequate map, and it is completely natural to feel overwhelmed. Deep down, you do not want a compliance-driven household where your child simply follows orders out of fear; you want a home of genuine connection and understanding. You long for those beautiful, quiet moments of shared joy, where your child looks at you with absolute trust, feeling completely safe in their own skin. You desire a practical daily routine that supports your child's unique developmental pacing while reducing the frequency and severity of exhausting meltdowns. Ultimately, your goal is to help your child develop genuine independence, social confidence, and emotional resilience so they can successfully navigate the world on their own terms. This book is designed to show you that this hopeful future is entirely within your reach. A beautiful shift occurs when we stop trying to fix behavioral symptoms and start addressing the sensory and emotional needs driving them. By embracing a connection-first framework, you can cultivate a home environment where meltdowns naturally decrease because your child feels deeply understood and neurologically safe. You will move away from the exhausting role of a constant behavior-tracker and step into the role of an intuitive, supportive guide. This approach does not require you to tolerate destructive behavior, but rather empowers you to understand the *sensory and emotional why* behind your child's distress. As you learn to read their subtle cues, you will establish a deep sense of mutual trust that serves as the engine for all developmental progress. Instead of managing your household with rigid reward charts, compliance metrics, and constant disciplinary friction, you can establish a calm, predictable home environment built on intuitive connection. You will no longer need to rely on compliance-driven tactics that leave both you and your child feeling drained and disconnected at the end of the day. This shift allows your family to replace daily power struggles with compassionate behavior shifts that honor your child's unique nervous system. As your child's sensory and emotional needs are consistently met, you will notice a significant reduction in household tension. The constant state of hyper-vigilance will give way to a peaceful home where everyone can finally breathe a sigh of relief. By adopting this supportive framework, you will witness your child naturally reaching developmental milestones without the exhausting friction of constant behavioral policing. You will gain the confidence to handle unpredictable behavioral moments with calm assurance, knowing exactly how to de-escalate tension before it turns into a meltdown. This guidance offers you a clear, sustainable path forward, freeing you from the heavy burden of parental guilt, self-doubt, and fear. Your relationship with your child will deepen as you learn to celebrate their unique strengths rather than pathologizing their differences. You are about to build a home environment where your child can truly thrive, growing emotionally, socially, and behaviorally at their own beautiful pace. My journey into this space began not in a quiet clinical lecture hall, but in the chaotic trenches of my own home, holding my sobbing child while realizing that my master's degree in Applied Behavior Analysis had not prepared me for the raw reality of autistic parenting. Despite my training in behavioral modification, standard compliance-driven strategies fell short in our daily family life. I struggled with the same heavy guilt, sleepless nights, and endless questioning that you are likely experiencing right now. It was only when I began merging my professional behavioral insights with a heart-centered, supportive approach that our home began to experience true healing and progress. Through years of navigating both the scientific literature and my own household struggles, I discovered that true developmental growth cannot be forced through behavioral manipulation. This realization led to a breakthrough in my professional practice, shifting my focus toward neurodiversity-affirming habits and intuitive family connection. I realized that our children do not need to be fixed or forced to fit into a neurotypical mold; instead, they need us to understand their unique nervous systems and build a secure developmental bridge. Combining my clinical expertise with my lived experience as a mother allowed me to create a practical, heart-centered framework that actually works in the middle of a busy, messy household. As a developmental specialist who lives this reality every single day, I designed this guide to bridge the gap between clinical research and lived household experience. My mission is to offer you the gentle reassurance, professional authority, and actionable tools you need to foster a nurturing home environment. I have walked this exact path, and I know how incredibly lonely and exhausting it can feel without the right support. By sharing the lessons I have learned both as a professional and a mother, I hope to save you years of trial and error, guiding you toward a parenting style that feels hopeful instead of fear-based. Throughout the upcoming chapters, we will explore the core tenets of the Ascent Framework, a unique developmental path that prioritizes emotional attunement and natural progression. You will discover how to look beyond the surface of your child's behavior, decoding the complex sensory processing differences that shape their daily reality. We will explore the mechanics of emotional dysregulation, helping you understand how to distinguish between a behavioral tantrum and a genuine sensory meltdown. By mastering these concepts, you will build a solid foundation for supporting your child's emotional balance with compassion instead of control. You will master the art of intuitive observation, learning how to decode subtle non-verbal signals and body language before your child reaches the point of distress. This guide provides you with practical, daily routines that seamlessly fit into your existing household schedule, turning everyday moments like mealtimes and play into opportunities for deep connection. You will learn to use sensory-friendly communication strategies and visual aids that reduce your child's daily anxiety and support their natural desire for autonomy. These tools are designed to be highly actionable, offering you clear, step-by-step guidance that you can begin implementing in your home today. Our focus will be on establishing neurodiversity-affirming habits that respect your child's unique pacing and sensory profile. You will gain access to specific grounding techniques to maintain your own calm during periods of escalation, creating a stable environment for effective de-escalation. We will discuss gentle, reflective strategies to rebuild connection and trust with your child after a meltdown, ensuring that difficult moments become opportunities for relational growth. Additionally, this guide offers mindset-based exercises specifically designed to help you release parental guilt and build sustainable self-compassion. You will learn to measure progress not by societal expectations, but by the quiet, meaningful victories that occur within your own home. Please take a deep breath and let go of the impossible expectation of being a perfect parent. This developmental journey does not require you to have all the answers, nor does it demand flawless execution of every strategy. What your child needs most is not a perfect parent, but an attuned, compassionate advocate who is willing to listen, connect, and grow alongside them. You are already the parent your child needs, and your willingness to seek new pathways is a beautiful testament to your love. Let us set aside the weight of societal judgment and step forward with a renewed sense of confidence, hope, and reassurance. Let us begin this ascent together, turning away from the exhausting cycle of behavioral modification and moving toward a home filled with genuine connection, understanding, and joy. Each step we take together will bring you closer to a calmer household, a deeper bond with your child, and a sustainable sense of confidence in your parenting. The path ahead is not about changing who your child is, but about celebrating their unique mind while providing the secure foundation they need to reach new heights. Open your heart to the possibilities of this supportive framework, and let us embark on this transformative parenting journey today.

1

WHY CONNECTION MATTERS MORE THAN COMPLIANCE

✦

EMBRACING THE CONNECTION-FIRST MINDSET

Redefining Success for Growth

When I asked parents in my practice to define what progress looked like for their child, most started with behaviors: fewer tantrums, better compliance, sitting still at the dinner table. And I understood completely—those visible milestones feel like proof that something is working. But what if we've been measuring the wrong things all along?

Traditional parenting advice often centers on managing behaviors, treating each meltdown or refusal as a problem to solve (Delahooke, 2019). The underlying message? Your child needs to fit into the world as it is. But this compliance-first approach misses something fundamental: your child isn't broken, and connection—not conformity—is what unlocks true developmental growth (Desautels, 2020)..

Shifting to a connection-first mindset means redefining success entirely. Instead of asking, "Did my child comply today?" you might ask, "Did we understand each other a little better? Did I notice what triggered their overwhelm before it escalated?" Progress becomes less about external behaviors and more about the quality of your relationship and your child's internal sense of safety.

This isn't just a feel-good philosophy. When your child feels genuinely seen and supported, their nervous system settles (Delahooke, 2022). They become more open to learning, communicating, and navigating the world. The behaviors you were chasing often improve naturally—not because you demanded compliance, but because you addressed the underlying needs driving those behaviors.

Your child's developmental journey is entirely their own, unfolding at their own pace and in their own way. By letting go of rigid milestones and embracing the unique path ahead, you create space for authentic growth. You stop fighting against your child's wiring and start working *with* it, building trust that becomes the foundation for everything else (Reber, 2018).

Connection isn't a detour from progress—it is the progress.

Understanding Connection as a Core Principle

Connection-first parenting means treating your relationship with your child as the primary tool for growth, not a secondary consideration once behaviors are managed. It is a deliberate shift in how you interpret your child's signals and responses throughout the day.

When your child refuses to put on their shoes, a compliance-focused response targets the behavior: "You need to listen when I ask you to do something." A connection-first response asks a different question: "What's making this hard for them right now?" Maybe the socks feel wrong, maybe the transition from home to car feels overwhelming, or maybe they're still processing something that happened an hour ago. Connection means pausing to understand the need beneath the behavior before jumping to correction.

This approach rests on a simple but powerful premise: children do well when they can (Greene, 2014). Challenging behaviors aren't manipulation or defiance—they're communication. Your child is showing you, often in the only way they know how, that something isn't working. When you respond with curiosity instead of control, you are building what developmental specialists call *co-regulation*—the process of lending your calm, regulated nervous system to help your child find theirs (Shanker, 2016) (Shanker, 2016). (Greene, 2014)

Co-regulation does not mean permissiveness or avoiding boundaries. It means recognizing that your child cannot access problem-solving, flexibility, or self-control when their nervous system is in distress. Over time, this changes everything. Your child begins to trust that you are safe, and that you won't punish them for struggles they cannot yet manage. That trust creates space for genuine learning and growth—the kind that lasts because it is built on understanding, not fear.

You stop seeing meltdowns as failures and start seeing them as valuable information about what your child needs. The behaviors you were chasing often shift naturally when connection becomes your foundation, because you are finally addressing what was driving them all along.

Practical Mindset Shifts for Parents

When you shift to connection-first parenting, you're doing more than reducing tantrums or smoothing out bedtime routines. You're protecting something deeper: your child's sense of self.

Research from the Center on the Developing Child at Harvard demonstrates that prolonged stress—especially stress rooted in feeling misunderstood or unsafe—can disrupt the developing brain's architecture (National Scientific Council on the Developing Child, 2014). For autistic children, who already navigate a world demanding constant adaptation, this matters profoundly. Every time you respond with curiosity instead of correction, you're affirming that your child's internal experience is valid, not wrong, not broken, not something to be trained away.

Most parents aren't worried about theory. They're worried about right now.

They're worried about their child who won't go to school without a two-hour meltdown, the sibling who feels invisible, the job they might lose if they're late again. Connection-first parenting addresses those immediate pressures while also breaking the cycle of shame that many autistic children internalize early. When compliance becomes the goal, children learn that their worth depends on how well they can mask, perform, or push through distress. That lesson doesn't fade—it compounds.

A study in the *Journal of Autism and Developmental Disorders* found that autistic adults who experienced higher levels of acceptance reported significantly lower symptoms of depression and stress (Cage et al., 2018). Connection is preventative care for your child's long-term mental health.

What you do now shapes not just how your child behaves, but how they feel about themselves at fifteen, twenty-five, or forty. You're building the foundation for a life where they trust their own needs, ask for help without shame, and believe they deserve relationships built on understanding rather than endurance. That foundation starts with small moments—shoe refusals, bedtime struggles, grocery store meltdowns—where you choose to see your child, not just manage them.

THE LIMITATIONS OF COMPLIANCE-BASED STRATEGIES

Understanding Compliance Pitfalls

When compliance becomes the primary goal, we often miss the most important question: why is this happening? That resistance to sitting at the table might stem from scratchy chair fabric or fluorescent lights humming overhead. The screaming during transitions could signal genuine terror when familiar patterns shift unexpectedly. Compliance-driven approaches treat these moments as behavioral problems requiring correction through rewards or consequences, completely bypassing what your child is actually experiencing.

Sure, you might see short-term change. Your child sits because they want the reward. But you haven't addressed the sensory overload or emotional distress that triggered the original response in the first place.

Over time, this approach creates a troubling pattern. Children learn that their internal experiences matter less than their external performance. They discover that expressing discomfort, fear, or overwhelm leads to correction rather than understanding. The message becomes clear: your feelings are less important than appearing calm and cooperative. This dynamic erodes the very foundation we're trying to build—a relationship where your child feels safe communicating their genuine needs.

The compliance framework also places enormous pressure on parents. You become enforcers rather than allies, constantly monitoring behavior charts and tracking whether rewards are working. The relationship shifts from connection to transaction, from understanding to management. Both you and your child end up exhausted, locked in a cycle that prioritizes appearance over authentic growth.

What gets lost is trust. When children repeatedly experience their distress being managed rather than understood, they stop turning to parents for support. They learn to mask their struggles or shut down entirely. The very behaviors we're trying to address often intensify because the underlying causes remain unaddressed, building pressure beneath a compliant surface.

There's another way forward—one that honors both your child's experience and your deep desire to help them thrive.

Shifting Towards Connection

Traditional compliance-based approaches often focus on what your child *should* do, without pausing to ask *why* they're struggling in the first place. When your child resists homework, the instinct might be to enforce stricter rules or offer bigger rewards. But what if the real issue isn't defiance—it's something sensory, emotional, or environmental that you haven't uncovered yet? (Delahooke, 2019)

Start by inviting dialogue instead of demanding action. Try saying, "I want to understand what makes this tough for you," and then genuinely wait. Silence can be uncomfortable, but it creates space for your child to process and respond. If articulating feelings is hard, offer gentle prompts: "Does the work feel too long? Too confusing? Is something else bothering you when we sit down?" Some children express themselves more clearly through drawing, pointing to emotion cards, or choosing between pictures that represent how they feel.

Once you've identified the real barrier—maybe your child loses focus after ten minutes, or the lighting in the room feels overwhelming—you can collaborate on meaningful solutions. Ask, "What if we broke this into two shorter sessions with a movement break in between? Or used a timer so you know exactly when you're done?" Let your child contribute their own ideas. When they help design the solution, they're far more likely to engage with it.

This shift from compliance to collaboration doesn't just solve the immediate problem. It builds trust, teaches problem-solving, and shows your child that their internal experience matters more than outward obedience. Over time, this connection-first approach leads to deeper developmental progress and a relationship rooted in mutual respect—not fear or frustration. (Greene, 2021)

THE TRANSFORMATIVE POWER OF UNDERSTANDING

Empathy as a Foundation

Empathy begins when you pause to wonder what your child's experience actually feels like. Not what the behavior looks like from the outside—but what it feels like from the inside, a shift in perspective central to what psychologists call parental reflective functioning (Slade, 2005). When your child melts down in a crowded grocery store, compliance-based thinking asks, "How do I stop this?" Empathy asks, "What is overwhelming them right now?"

That shift changes everything.

Seeing the world through your child's eyes means recognizing that a fluorescent-lit aisle isn't just bright—it might feel like standing under a spotlight that hums and flickers unpredictably. A simple request to "hurry up" isn't just instruction—it might land like urgent pressure when their brain is already working overtime to process sounds, sights, and transitions. When you start to imagine the sensory and emotional weight your child carries moment to moment, your responses naturally soften, especially as research shows a strong link between a child's sensory processing difficulties, behavioral issues, and increased parenting stress (Gourley et al., 2013). You move from correcting behavior to supporting a nervous system under strain.

This perspective doesn't excuse difficult moments, but it reframes them. Instead of seeing defiance, you might see a child whose body is saying "too much." Instead of labeling a reaction as dramatic, you recognize genuine distress. Empathy transforms your lens—and when your lens changes, so does your child's sense of safety with you.

Building this muscle takes practice, but it starts simply: pause before reacting, breathe, and ask yourself what might be true for them in this moment.

Understanding Sensory Experiences

Start with observation. Notice what your child seeks out and what they avoid. Do they gravitate toward weighted blankets or tight hugs? Do they cover their ears in certain rooms? Write it down—not to diagnose, but to detect patterns that reveal their unique sensory profile (Dunn, 1999)., aligned with established clinical models like *Winnie Dunn's Sensory Processing Framework*.

Once you've identified a few consistent responses, test small adjustments. If your child struggles during meals, consider the chair's texture, the table's height, or background noise from appliances. Change one variable at a time so you can track what actually helps. This methodical approach prevents overwhelm and builds your confidence as you learn what works.

Create a sensory audit of your home, inspired by environmental tools from the Autism Education Trust (AET, 2016). Inspired by environmental tools from the *Autism Education Trust*, walk through each room and notice lighting—is it harsh overhead fluorescence or softer lamps? Check for persistent sounds: refrigerator hum, ticking clocks, air vents. Feel fabric textures on furniture and clothing. Smell cleaning products, air fresheners, or cooking odors that linger.

Your child experiences all of this, often simultaneously, without the ability to filter or ignore what neurotypical nervous systems dismiss automatically.

Build a "sensory toolkit" together. Include items that regulate: noise-canceling headphones, sunglasses for bright environments, fidget tools for tactile input, chewy necklaces for oral sensory needs. Let your child choose what feels right—their preferences matter more than expert recommendations. One child might find a soft stuffed animal soothing while another needs something with more resistance, like a textured ball.

Communicate your understanding through action, not just words. When you dim lights without being asked, when you warn before vacuuming, when you cut tags from shirts before they're worn

—these small gestures tell your child you see them. You're learning their language.

The framework itself is simple: observe, adjust, validate, repeat. But the impact extends far beyond sensory comfort. When children feel understood at this fundamental level—when their physical experience of the world is acknowledged and accommodated—they begin to trust that you're truly on their side.

Decoding Emotional Signals

You'll miss signals sometimes. You'll misread a cue, offer the wrong support, or completely overlook what your child needed in the moment. This isn't failure—research by developmental psychologist Ed Tronick shows that even well-attuned caregivers are out of sync with their children about 70% of the time (Tronick & Cohn, 1989).. What builds resilience is the cycle of interactive repair.

When you realize you've misunderstood, say so. "I thought you needed space, but I see now you wanted help. I'm still learning how to read what you need." This honesty builds trust far more effectively than pretending you got it right. Your child learns that repair is possible, that relationships can withstand mistakes.

Start by observing without judgment. Notice when your child's shoulders tense during transitions, or when their eyes dart toward the door before a meltdown. These physical shifts—tightened fists, shallow breathing, fidgeting hands—are your child's body communicating distress before words can form. The goal isn't perfect interpretation every time. It's building a practice of gentle curiosity.

Keep a simple mental note of patterns. Does your child become quieter when overwhelmed, or louder? Do they seek you out or withdraw? Over time, these observations form a map of your child's unique emotional language. You're not guessing blindly—you're learning to read the signals that have always been there.

Trust what you notice, even when it contradicts what you've been told to expect. Your child might smile during distress, or melt down hours after a triggering event. Autistic emotional expression doesn't always follow neurotypical timelines or presentations (Brewer et al., 2016). Your attunement to *your* child matters more than any generalized checklist.

When you respond to subtle cues early—offering a sensory break before the crying starts, validating frustration before it escalates—you're teaching your child that their internal experiences matter. You're building a foundation where communication flows both ways, rooted in mutual understanding rather than compliance.

Practical Understanding in Daily Life

Progress doesn't arrive in neat increments. Some weeks you'll feel like you're finally getting it—you'll recognize your child's distress signal before it escalates, offer the right support, and watch tension dissolve. Other weeks you'll feel like you're starting from scratch, misreading everything, exhausted and discouraged.

Both experiences are normal. Understanding your child isn't a skill you master and check off. It's an ongoing practice that shifts as your child grows, as environments change, as new stressors emerge. What worked brilliantly last month might stop working tomorrow, not because you're failing but because your child is developing.

When you feel stuck, resist the urge to overhaul everything at once. Pick one small interaction—bedtime, snack time, the transition from school to home—and bring your full attention there. Notice what happens in your child's body and voice during that specific moment. This focused observation often reveals patterns you miss when trying to monitor everything simultaneously.

Common obstacles will surface repeatedly. You'll forget to pause before reacting. You'll slip back into directing rather than collaborating, especially when you're tired or overwhelmed yourself. Your child will resist your attempts to understand, particularly if previous approaches felt invasive or corrective. They might need time to trust that you genuinely want to know their experience rather than fix their behavior.

Give yourself permission to be learning alongside your child. You don't need perfect attunement every time. You need willingness to keep trying, to repair when you miss the mark, to stay curious even when you're exhausted. Research consistently shows that the parent's capacity for self-compassion directly impacts their ability to respond flexibly to their child's needs. When you're harsh with yourself about mistakes, that rigidity spills into your interactions.

Some days, understanding will feel impossible. Your child's distress will overwhelm you both, and you won't know what they need. That's when you lean on what you do know: your presence matters. Staying regulated yourself, offering reassurance without demanding resolution, models emotional safety even when you can't solve the immediate problem.

Progress shows up in unexpected moments—your child seeking you out during stress instead of withdrawing, expressing a need before melting down, trusting you enough to show vulnerability. These shifts won't announce themselves. You'll notice them later, realizing something fundamental has changed in how you move through hard moments together.

2

UNDERSTANDING YOUR CHILD'S NERVOUS SYSTEM AND SENSORY NEEDS

✦

DECODING SENSORY PROCESSING: THE BASICS

Understanding Sensory Processing

When a child clamps their hands over their ears in a grocery store, the behavior isn't defiance. The fluorescent lights buzz at a frequency most adults tune out automatically, but for many autistic children, that hum arrives in the brain without any filter—raw, overwhelming, and impossible to ignore. What looks like a meltdown is actually a nervous system in distress, flooded with sensory information it cannot process efficiently.

Sensory processing is the brain's ongoing task of receiving, organizing, and interpreting information from the environment. Touch, sound, sight, smell, taste—plus less obvious inputs like balance and body position—stream into the nervous system constantly. Research shows that up to 96% of autistic individuals experience sensory processing differences (Kilroy et al., 2019) (Kilroy et al., 2019). While a neurotypical brain acts like a skilled editor, highlighting what matters and dimming background noise, an autistic brain often experiences this editing process differently.

Some sensory inputs arrive *amplified*, as if the volume knob is permanently turned too high. Others barely register at all, leaving a child craving more input just to feel grounded.

This isn't a matter of preference or temperament—it is a physical reality of their neurology. When sensory systems do not integrate smoothly, everyday environments become unpredictable. A clothing tag transforms into a sharp jab, the smell of cooking triggers nausea, and wet grass underfoot registers as pain rather than texture. These aren't exaggerations or attention-seeking behaviors—they are authentic experiences shaped by how the nervous system interprets stimuli.

Understanding this distinction changes everything. Behaviors that once seemed manipulative begin to make sense when you recognize the nervous system's role. Your child isn't being difficult when they refuse certain fabrics or insist on the same meal daily; they are responding to genuine sensory discomfort their brain cannot easily modulate.

The challenge is that sensory processing differences vary dramatically, even among autistic children. One child might seek constant movement while another freezes in overstimulation. One craves deep pressure while another recoils from the lightest touch. There's no universal sensory profile, which means understanding *your* child's specific nervous system becomes essential.

Identifying Sensory Preferences

Sensory preferences shift constantly—reshaped by context, energy levels, and a dozen variables that make any single day feel unpredictable. A child who typically tolerates loud noises might completely unravel when tired, hungry, or already managing discomfort from an itchy sweater. The same swing that brought joy yesterday might trigger panic today if their *vestibular system*—the sensory system responsible for balance and spatial orientation—is already overwhelmed.

First popularized in Dr. Winnie Dunn's model of sensory processing, sensory seeking describes the drive for more neurological input (Dunn, 1997). These children might crash into furniture, spin endlessly, chew on shirt collars, or crave tight hugs. Their nervous systems have high thresholds for stimulation, requiring intense sensory inputs to register sensation and feel regulated. Conversely, sensory avoiding represents an active strategy to limit overwhelming stimuli. Children who avoid sensory input may cover their ears, refuse certain textures, resist light touch, or experience distress in crowded spaces. Because their neurological thresholds are incredibly low, they instinctively withdraw from environments that feel unbearable. (Dunn, 1997)

Most children do not fall neatly into one category.

Your child might seek deep pressure through bear hugs but avoid light touch on their arms. They might crave spinning but panic when their feet leave the ground. They might love crunchy foods but refuse anything mushy. These contradictions are not inconsistencies—they reflect the complexity of how different sensory systems operate independently within the same body.

Recognizing these patterns requires observation, not diagnosis. Watch what your child gravitates toward and what they avoid. Notice when meltdowns happen and what sensory factors might have contributed. Does your child struggle more in the morning when getting dressed, or in the evening when exhausted? Do they calm down after jumping on the couch, or do they need quiet and dimmed lights?

The goal is not to eliminate all discomfort—that would be impossible. The goal is to understand the sensory landscape your child navigates daily so you can make small, meaningful adjustments that reduce unnecessary strain. This might mean cutting tags from shirts, offering noise-canceling headphones before entering a loud space, or building in movement breaks throughout the day. It might mean recognizing that your child's refusal to wear certain shoes is not stubbornness but genuine physical discomfort their brain cannot ignore.

Every child's sensory profile is as unique as their fingerprint.

Strategies for Sensory Support

Sensory overwhelm doesn't announce itself politely. It shows up as a screaming meltdown in the grocery store, a refusal to leave the house, or a child who cannot focus at school because the fluorescent lights feel like needles against their skin. When you understand that these moments are neurological realities rather than behavioral choices, the entire framing shifts. Your child is not being difficult—they are experiencing genuine physical distress that their developing nervous system cannot yet regulate independently.

Research consistently demonstrates that unaddressed sensory processing differences correlate with heightened anxiety, emotional dysregulation, and significant impairments in daily functioning (Ben-Sasson et al., 2009). Children who experience chronic sensory overload exist in a near-constant state of stress, their bodies flooded with cortisol and adrenaline. This physiological response is not metaphorical—it is measurable, observable, and profoundly impactful on development. When a child's nervous system remains in survival mode, learning, social connection, and emotional regulation become secondary priorities. The brain simply cannot prioritize growth when it perceives threat.

The stakes extend beyond individual moments of distress.

Over time, repeated sensory overwhelm shapes how children perceive the world and their place within it. A child who consistently feels bombarded by sensory input may begin to view new environments as inherently dangerous, developing avoidance patterns that limit social participation and learning opportunities. They might stop trying new foods, refuse playdates, or resist school entirely—not from defiance, but from a legitimate need to protect themselves from experiences their nervous system cannot safely process. Without support, these protective strategies can narrow a child's world considerably.

Yet when parents gain tools to recognize and respond to sensory needs proactively, the trajectory changes. Studies on *sensory integration therapy* and environmental modifications show measurable improvements in self-regulation, participation in daily activities, and overall quality of life (Schaaf et al., 2018) (Schaaf et al., 2018). These outcomes matter because they represent more than behavioral compliance—they reflect a child's growing capacity to engage with their environment without constant distress. A child who receives appropriate sensory support can participate in family dinners, tolerate necessary medical appointments, and explore new experiences without their nervous system constantly signaling danger.

This is not about creating a perfectly controlled environment where discomfort never exists. That goal would be both impossible and counterproductive. Rather, it is about reducing unnecessary sensory strain so your child has the neurological bandwidth to develop coping skills, build resilience, and engage meaningfully with the world. When a child is not constantly battling sensory overload, they have more capacity for connection, learning, and joy.

The difference between a child who receives sensory support and one who does not is not trivial. It shapes their relationship with their own body, their willingness to engage with new experiences, and their fundamental sense of safety in the world.

EMOTIONAL REGULATION AND ITS HIDDEN CHALLENGES

Understanding Emotional Dysregulation

When your child screams at the birthday party and won't explain why, when they throw the crayon box during a perfectly calm afternoon, when they dissolve into tears because dinner is chicken instead of pasta—these aren't necessarily tantrums. Often, they're signs of emotional dysregulation: the brain's inability to manage the intensity, duration, or expression of emotional responses (Gross, 1998).

Emotional regulation involves recognizing what you feel, assessing its appropriateness to the situation, and modulating your response accordingly. It's the capacity to feel disappointment without collapsing, frustration without lashing out, excitement without spiraling into chaos. For many autistic children, this process doesn't work smoothly —not because they lack willpower or discipline, but because their neurological wiring processes emotions differently.

The brain's emotional regulation system depends on several interconnected structures: the amygdala detects threats and triggers emotional responses, while the prefrontal cortex evaluates context and applies brakes when needed. Research shows these systems develop differently in autistic individuals, with variations in functional connectivity patterns between these regions (Swartz et al., 2013). When emotional input floods in faster than the brain can evaluate it, dysregulation follows. A minor disappointment—running out of apple juice—triggers the same physiological response as genuine danger. The emotional volume dial gets stuck at maximum, with no middle settings available. Your child isn't choosing this intensity; they're experiencing it as overwhelmingly real.

Here's what makes it particularly challenging: emotional dysregulation looks exactly like deliberate misbehavior. Both involve yelling, throwing objects, refusing cooperation, melting down. But the underlying causes differ completely.

Misbehavior involves conscious choice—testing boundaries, seeking attention, avoiding tasks. Dysregulation involves neurological overwhelm—the brain temporarily losing capacity to process and manage emotional intensity. When you interpret dysregulation as defiance, interventions fail predictably. Consequences, time-outs, and stern lectures don't help a child whose amygdala is flooding their system with stress hormones. They need co-regulation and safety, not discipline.

Most autistic children can't articulate what's happening internally. They don't recognize the building pressure before eruption, can't name the specific emotion driving their reaction, and struggle to connect their physical sensations to emotional states (Shah et al., 2016). This makes prevention and intervention feel impossible—until you learn to read the patterns yourself.

Identifying Triggers and Patterns

Maya's parents brought her in after three weeks of daily meltdowns. She was seven, verbal, and doing well academically—but every afternoon around 3:30, she'd explode. Screaming, throwing toys, remaining inconsolable for thirty to forty minutes. Her parents had tried everything: earlier bedtimes, different snacks, rewards charts, consequences.

Nothing worked.

I asked them to track one week without changing anything. Just observe and document: What happened in the fifteen minutes before each meltdown? What was Maya doing? Where was she? What had she eaten? How much sleep had she gotten the night before?

The pattern emerged immediately. Every meltdown occurred on days when Maya's classroom had an afternoon assembly. The gymnasium's echoing acoustics, fluorescent lighting, and packed bleachers created sensory overload that Maya's nervous system couldn't process in the moment. She'd hold herself together at school—masking her distress and suppressing her mounting overwhelm—then collapse the instant she felt safe at home. Her parents were seeing the aftermath, not the trigger.

This phenomenon, sometimes called after-school restraint collapse, is common in autistic children who spend hours managing sensory and social demands that exceed their neurological capacity (Raymaker et al., 2020). The child isn't being manipulative; they're finally releasing the immense cognitive and sensory pressure that has built up all day.

Effective observation requires specificity. "She had a bad day" doesn't help. "She had gym class with whistles blowing, then library time where she couldn't find her favorite book, then missed snack because the line was too long" gives you workable information. Keep a simple tracking log for one week—date, time, activity before the meltdown, sensory environment, and any physical needs like hunger or fatigue. You're not diagnosing. You're becoming a detective in your child's daily experience, learning the language their nervous system speaks when words fall short.

Once you spot the patterns, interventions become intuitive. Maya's parents started picking her up early on assembly days and scheduling sensory breaks immediately after school. Within two weeks, the afternoon explosions stopped. Not because Maya changed, but because her parents learned to read what her body was trying to tell them all along.

Tools for Supporting Emotional Balance

Before implementing any strategy, spend three full days simply observing. Notice when your child seems calm versus when they're edging toward overload. Watch for the small tells: stimming that intensifies, voice pitch rising, decreased eye contact, rigid body language. These are your early warning signals—your child's nervous system communicating before words become impossible.

Creating a sensory break space in your home doesn't require elaborate equipment or extensive redesign. A corner with soft pillows, a weighted blanket, noise-canceling headphones, and dimmed lighting works for many children. Some need a compression tunnel or mini-trampoline. Others prefer a cardboard box they can crawl into. Let your child help choose what feels regulating—their body knows what it needs far better than any generic checklist.

Schedule proactive breaks rather than waiting for meltdowns. If your child typically struggles after school, build in twenty minutes of sensory decompression before anything else—no homework, no questions about their day, no transitions into the next activity.

Think of it like preventive medicine: you wouldn't wait until someone collapses from dehydration to offer water.

Emotional coaching during calm moments builds capacity for later regulation. When your child is regulated, practice naming feelings together. "I notice when you're frustrated, your hands make fists. When you're overwhelmed, you cover your ears. What does your body do when you're happy?" This metacognitive awareness—understanding their own internal states—becomes the foundation for self-regulation. You cannot teach these skills during a meltdown when the thinking brain has gone offline.

Develop a simple co-regulation routine. Bruce Perry's work on the autonomic nervous system emphasizes that *rhythm* regulates (Perry & Winfrey, 2021). Rocking, walking, swinging, even breathing in sync with your child activates the parasympathetic nervous system. A parent might sit beside their child during dysregulation, matching their breathing rhythm and then gradually slowing their own rate. Within minutes, the child's breathing unconsciously synchronizes and decelerates. (Perry & Winfrey, 2021)

When meltdowns happen—and they will—your goal isn't to stop them. Trying to halt a nervous system in full survival mode is like trying to stop a physical reflex mid-trigger. Instead, ensure safety first: remove harmful objects, create space, stay nearby without demands or eye contact. Your calm, grounded presence communicates safety even when words cannot reach them. Speak minimally, move slowly, keep your own nervous system regulated.

Children co-regulate off the adults around them.

After the storm passes, resist the urge to immediately debrief or discipline. The nervous system needs recovery time. Offer water, a preferred sensory activity, or simply quiet proximity. Wait at least an hour—sometimes longer—before gently discussing what happened, and only if your child has the capacity for that conversation.

Track what works. Keep brief notes: "Deep pressure for ten minutes before transitions—no meltdown today" or "Skipped sensory break—difficult afternoon." Patterns emerge slowly, but they do emerge. This isn't about perfection; it's about slowly building a library of what helps your specific child find their way back to calm.

MOVING BEYOND TRADITIONAL EXPECTATIONS

Redefining Success Metrics

Start by listing what you currently expect from your child. Write it down, honestly. Are you hoping they'll make eye contact during conversations? Sit still at restaurants? Participate in typical birthday parties? Play cooperatively with siblings? Excel in traditional classroom settings? These expectations often arrive before we even meet our children—inherited from parenting books, pediatrician milestones, and what we observe in other families.

Now comes the harder part: beside each expectation, note whether it reflects your child's neurology or someone else's definition of normal.

Does your child actually *want* extended eye contact, or does it genuinely cause discomfort (Hadjikhani et al., 2017)? Is classroom participation energizing or exhausting for their specific nervous system? This distinction changes everything. When we chase milestones designed for neurotypical development, we often inadvertently communicate to our child that who they are isn't quite right. That the way they naturally move through the world needs fixing. But when we pause to examine where these expectations truly come from, we create space for something far more powerful: personalized growth markers that celebrate your child's actual progress.

Consider what success might look like through a neurodiversity-affirming lens. Perhaps it's your child finding *their* comfortable way to show connection—a gentle hand squeeze instead of eye contact. Maybe it's building stamina for one meaningful social interaction rather than surviving an overwhelming birthday party. It could be discovering the learning environment where their mind genuinely thrives, whether that's a quiet corner with headphones or a sensory-rich outdoor space.

These aren't lowered expectations. They're recalibrated ones—adjusted to honor your child's unique wiring while still fostering genuine development and connection.

The relief that comes from this shift is profound, both for you and your child. You're no longer battling against their neurology, trying to force square pegs into round holes. Instead, you're becoming a keen observer of *their* path forward, noticing the small victories that actually matter: increased regulation, deeper trust, moments of joy, expanding comfort zones on their terms. This is where the real ascent begins—not toward someone else's summit, but toward your child's fullest, most authentic expression of themselves.

Embracing Neurodiversity

Most parents spend years measuring their child against developmental charts designed for entirely different brains before realizing they've been using the wrong ruler. That realization can feel disorienting—if the milestones we've been chasing don't apply, what exactly are we aiming for?

But this uncertainty eventually gives way to something steadier: the recognition that your child has been showing you their own markers of growth all along. When you stop asking your child to perform neurotypical behaviors and start noticing what they're actually communicating, patterns emerge. The way they've developed elaborate systems for organizing their collections shows executive functioning at work, just expressed differently. Their intense focus on specific topics reveals a capacity for deep learning that many adults spend lifetimes trying to cultivate.

The questions they ask—the ones that seem off-topic or oddly timed—often demonstrate a sophisticated understanding of abstract concepts that neurotypical peers haven't begun to grasp.

Shifting to a neurodiversity-affirming perspective means recognizing these strengths as genuine developmental achievements, not consolation prizes. Your child's ability to notice patterns others miss, their honest communication style, their passionate dedication to their interests—these aren't quirks to tolerate while waiting for "real" progress. They're the foundation of who your child is becoming.

This reframing changes everything about how you support their growth. Instead of trying to sand down the edges that make them different, you begin asking: *How can I help them build on these natural strengths?*

What environment allows these abilities to flourish? You start creating space for their intense interests rather than rationing them as rewards for compliance. You protect their need for predictability instead of forcing flexibility as a learning goal. You celebrate their direct communication rather than teaching them to obscure their meaning with social niceties that feel dishonest.

The practical strategies follow naturally from this mindset. When you notice your child's exceptional visual memory, you incorporate more visual supports into daily routines—not as accommodations for deficits, but as tools that match their learning style. When you recognize their need for movement isn't restlessness but genuine sensory regulation, you build movement breaks into the day as intentionally as mealtimes. When you understand their reluctance to make eye contact isn't rudeness but sensory overwhelm, you stop requesting it and discover how much more connected they become when that pressure lifts.

This approach doesn't mean ignoring areas where your child needs support.

It means understanding that true progress happens when we work with their neurology, not against it. The goal isn't to help them act more neurotypical. The goal is to help them become the fullest version of themselves—confident, regulated, and deeply connected to the people who matter most.

3

THE ASCENT FRAMEWORK: BUILDING PROGRESS THROUGH TRUST

INTRODUCING THE ASCENT FRAMEWORK

Understanding the Ascent Philosophy

When my daughter was four, her therapist said she'd made excellent progress. She was sitting in her chair during circle time now. Staying in line at dismissal. Following instructions without bolting for the door.

I nodded and thanked her, but I felt this uncomfortable twist in my chest.

Because at home, my daughter had stopped trying to tell me things. She'd point at the fridge and wait. She'd hand me her shoes without looking at me. When I asked what she wanted for lunch, she'd echo back my exact words—"what she wanted for lunch"—and stand there, silent.

The behaviors everyone was celebrating felt like a trade. She'd learned compliance, though clinical critiques highlight that an overemphasis on obedience in early intervention can suppress a child's authentic development and autonomy (Sandoval-Norton & Shkedy, 2019). But something else had gone quiet.

That realization changed everything for me. Not immediately—I didn't have language for it yet—but it planted a question I couldn't ignore. What if the goals we'd been chasing were leading us in the wrong direction? What if reducing visible distress wasn't the same as supporting actual development?

What if trust, connection, and her willingness to reach toward me mattered more than whether she sat still during circle time (Prizant & Fields-Meyer, 2015)?

The Ascent Framework was born from that question. It's built on the belief that meaningful progress doesn't come from shaping children into compliance, but from creating conditions where they feel safe enough to grow. Where *connection* becomes the foundation for everything else—communication, learning, resilience, joy.

Instead of measuring success by how well a child adapts to external expectations, we measure it by how deeply they trust us, how freely they express themselves, and how naturally they engage with the world around them.

Core Components of Ascent

The framework rests on three pillars that work together, not in isolation.

Trust-building comes first because nothing else holds without it. When a child trusts you, they're willing to try things that feel hard. They'll tolerate discomfort because they believe you won't push them past what they can handle. Trust isn't about obedience—it's about safety. It's your child knowing, deep in their bones, that you see them as they are and won't demand they become someone else to earn your approval. This takes time. It requires you to stop correcting every behavior that makes you uncomfortable and start noticing what your child is trying to communicate through those behaviors instead.

Emotional attunement is the second pillar. It means reading your child's internal state, not just their external actions. A meltdown isn't defiance—it's nervous system overload. Withdrawal isn't rudeness—it's self-protection. Attunement asks you to look beneath the surface and respond to what's actually happening inside your child, even when their behavior looks frustrating or confusing from the outside.

You can't attune if you're focused solely on compliance.

The third pillar is personalized pacing, which acknowledges that developmental timelines aren't universal. Your child isn't behind—they're on their own trajectory. Personalized pacing means you follow their readiness, not a chart or a curriculum. You offer opportunities without pressure. You celebrate small shifts that might not register on a standardized assessment but represent real growth for your child. One week it might be tolerating a new texture. Another week it's sharing a brief moment of joint attention during play. These moments matter because they reflect your child moving toward the world at a pace that feels safe to them.

These three elements create the conditions for genuine development, not manufactured compliance.

Implementing Ascent in Daily Life

Weaving the Ascent Framework into your daily life doesn't require a complete household overhaul. It starts with small, intentional moments—the kinds you're already experiencing but might not recognize as opportunities for deep connection and trust-building.

Play becomes your workshop. When your child stacks blocks or lines up toy cars, resist the urge to redirect toward "productive" play. Instead, join them in their world. Narrate what they're doing without judgment: "You're making such a careful line." Mirror their actions. Let them lead. This simple act of following their interests builds trust far more powerfully than any structured lesson ever could (Le Couteur et al., 2016).

Communication shifts when you pause before responding. Your child might grunt, point, or use a single word—honor that effort as real communication. Respond as if they've told you a complete thought: "Oh, you want the red cup! Let me get that for you." You're not correcting; you're modeling and validating. Over time, this responsive rhythm teaches them that their voice matters.

Transitions are where trust gets tested most. Before leaving the park, give a five-minute warning. Then a two-minute one. Crouch to their eye level and describe what's coming next: "We're going home now. You'll have your snack, then we'll read together." Predictability is kindness to a nervous system that craves order.

The framework isn't about perfection—it's about presence. Some days you'll forget the warning before a transition. Some days you'll feel too tired to get down on the floor. That's okay. Progress lives in the pattern, not the single moment. What matters is that you're building a foundation where your child knows: *My parent sees me. My parent hears me. I am safe here.*

CORE PRINCIPLES OF TRUST-BASED PROGRESS

Building Emotional Safety

Emotional safety isn't simply an absence of yelling or punishment. It's the felt experience in your child's body that tells them: here, with this person, I don't have to pretend.

When your daughter melts down because her banana broke, emotional safety means you don't rush to fix her feelings or explain why it doesn't matter. You sit nearby. You acknowledge what she's experiencing without minimizing it. "That really upset you. You wanted it whole." You don't need her to calm down faster to prove you're doing it right. Her nervous system learns something profound in that moment—that big feelings don't make her unacceptable.

This principle differs sharply from traditional behavioral approaches that view *dysregulation* as something to extinguish. Those methods often inadvertently teach children that certain emotions make adults uncomfortable, that authentic responses lead to correction or redirection. Over time, children learn to suppress rather than express, to mask rather than communicate.

Emotional safety requires that we stop treating our children's distress as problems to solve and start recognizing them as information.

When your son refuses to enter the grocery store, he's not being difficult. His nervous system is experiencing what neuroscientist Dr. Stephen Porges conceptualizes as neuroception—subconsciously determining, based on fluorescent lighting, overlapping voices, and the unpredictability of crowds, that this environment poses a threat (Porges, 2004). You create safety not by convincing him he's wrong, but by believing him. (Porges, 2004)

What happens next matters deeply. You might say, "Okay, this feels too hard right now. Let's figure out another way." Perhaps you shop during quiet hours next time, or he waits in the car with noise-canceling headphones while you grab three items instead of filling a cart. You're not surrendering to avoidance; you're honoring his accurate self-assessment while maintaining the relationship.

Children who experience consistent emotional safety develop something irreplaceable: the willingness to keep trying. They attempt new foods, unfamiliar social situations, challenging tasks—not because they've been trained into compliance, but because they trust that failure won't result in shame. They know you'll meet their struggles with curiosity rather than disappointment.

That trust becomes the foundation for every other kind of growth.

Fostering Consistent Routines

At six years old, Marcus would stand frozen in his kitchen doorway every morning, unable to move forward until his mother said exactly the same phrase she'd used the day before: "Good morning, buddy. Oatmeal's ready when you are." If she varied even one word—"Hey, sweetie" or "breakfast is ready"—he'd retreat to his room, overwhelmed.

His mother, Elena, initially found this exhausting. She felt trapped by invisible scripts she hadn't known she was writing. But her occupational therapist reframed it: Marcus wasn't being controlling. His nervous system was desperately seeking predictability in a world that felt chaotic and unreadable.

Research on autistic children, such as studies led by Dr. Blythe Corbett, demonstrates that predictability supports physiological regulation, while unexpected schedule changes trigger significant elevations in evening salivary cortisol. When children know what comes next, their brains can shift from threat-detection mode into a state where connection becomes possible. In *Uniquely Human*, Dr. Barry Prizant writes that "the opposite of anxiety is not calm, but trust," showing how predictability frees up cognitive resources.

Elena began structuring Marcus's mornings with deliberate consistency. Same greeting, same breakfast options presented in the same order, same transition sequence: eat, brush teeth, shoes, backpack. Within three weeks, something shifted. Marcus started lingering at breakfast, occasionally asking questions, making brief eye contact. The rigidity everyone had worried about wasn't the problem—it was the solution his nervous system needed.

Predictability isn't about control or rigidity for its own sake. It's about building a foundation stable enough that your child can redirect energy away from survival vigilance and toward growth.

When the scaffolding holds steady, they can risk stepping forward. That's when trust deepens into something actionable.

Encouraging Autonomy and Choice

Predictability creates safety. But if a child never makes choices, they remain perpetually dependent on someone else holding the map.

Autonomy doesn't mean total freedom or independence beyond a child's capacity. It means offering genuine choices within safe boundaries—decisions small enough to manage but meaningful enough to matter. When seven-year-old Jada's father started letting her choose between two breakfast options instead of simply serving oatmeal, she began approaching mornings with curiosity rather than resignation. The choice itself was minor. The message it sent was profound: *Your preferences exist. They're worth considering.*

Dr. Laura Schreibman's research on neurodivergent development and Naturalistic Developmental Behavioral Interventions (NDBIs) shows that choice-making is a core driver of self-regulation and cognitive flexibility (Schreibman et al., 2015). When children practice low-stakes decisions—blue cup or green cup, park or library, five more minutes or stop now—they're rehearsing agency. That rehearsal builds the internal sense that they can influence their world, which directly feeds trust.

But autonomy fails when choices overwhelm. Offering twelve shirt options to a child already dysregulated by morning light doesn't build confidence—it triggers shutdown.

The same goes for choices that aren't actually choices: "Do you want to brush your teeth?" when refusal isn't an option breeds resentment, not trust. Effective autonomy requires structure. Two clear options. Presented calmly. Honored consistently. If your child picks the blue cup, don't override it because the green one's cleaner. If they choose the park over the library, go to the park. When children learn their choices produce predictable outcomes, they begin trusting their own judgment.

And when a child trusts their judgment, they stop waiting for someone else to tell them who to be.

Emphasizing Empathy in Interactions

Start where you are. Tomorrow morning, before your child's first request, pause. Don't anticipate, don't preempt, don't solve before they've communicated a need. Just wait.

When they point at the cabinet, resist grabbing what you *think* they want. Instead, narrate what you notice: "You're pointing up high. Are you showing me something?" Then wait again. If they grunt, nod, or shift their gaze, you've received communication. Honor it by responding to their intent, not your assumption. This small loop—observe, reflect, wait, respond—is empathetic communication in its most essential form. It tells your child: *I'm not rushing you. I'm listening.*

Next, practice labeling emotions without fixing them. When your child melts down over a broken cracker, the instinct is to replace it immediately, erase the distress, move on. But empathy requires sitting with discomfort long enough to name it. "That cracker broke. You're really upset. You wanted it whole." You're not solving—you're witnessing. That witnessing builds trust because it proves you can tolerate their feelings without needing to make them disappear. (Lieberman et al., 2007)

Model empathy by narrating your own emotional experience aloud. When you're frustrated by spilled milk, say it: "I'm feeling overwhelmed right now. I need a breath." Your child learns that emotions are normal, nameable, and manageable—not shameful or dangerous. Over time, they'll internalize this rhythm and begin using it themselves, building the emotional vocabulary that strengthens connection and self-regulation (Gottman & DeClaire, 1997).

APPLYING THE FRAMEWORK IN DAILY LIFE

Integrating Trust-Building Rituals

When mealtimes roll around, resist the urge to turn them into therapy sessions. Instead, let them become quiet moments of togetherness—times when you're side by side, sharing space without demand. A predictable rhythm at the table, a familiar plate, even the same spot each evening: these small consistencies speak volumes to a nervous system that craves order (Spagnola & Fiese, 2007). You're not forcing conversation or eye contact. You're simply being present, offering your child the gift of knowing what to expect.

Bedtime holds similar power. A sequence that never shifts—bath, story, lights low, the same lullaby—creates a container of safety your child can relax into (Mindell & Williamson, 2018). Within that container, trust begins to grow. Not because you demanded it, but because you honored their need for predictability. These rituals aren't about compliance; they're about building a foundation where your child feels secure enough to eventually reach toward you.

The beauty of this approach? It doesn't require extra time or elaborate planning.

You're already eating dinner. You're already putting your child to bed. The shift happens in *how* you show up during those moments—calm, attuned, reliable. Over weeks and months, these small, repeatable actions accumulate into something much larger: a relational safety net that supports every other area of growth. Your child learns that you can be trusted, that the world has rhythms they can count on, and that connection doesn't come with strings attached. That's the ascent framework in action, woven seamlessly into the fabric of your everyday life.

Adapting to Sensory Needs

Real progress doesn't arrive with fanfare or follow the developmental charts hanging in the pediatrician's office. You won't wake up one morning to find your child suddenly tolerating crowded grocery stores, maintaining extended eye contact, or transitioning between activities without resistance. Change unfolds in increments so subtle they're easy to miss if you're scanning for dramatic transformation.

Maybe your child lingered three seconds longer at breakfast before retreating to their room. Maybe they touched a new food with one finger instead of refusing to be near the plate. Maybe they tolerated the vacuum running in a different room when last month they needed it turned off entirely.

These moments don't announce themselves with fanfare, and

they certainly don't follow a linear trajectory. Some weeks you'll notice subtle shifts; other weeks you'll wonder if you've lost ground. Both are normal. Both are part of the process. The real obstacle isn't your child's pace—it's our cultural obsession with measurable milestones. We've been conditioned to expect progress reports, percentile rankings, developmental checklists that confirm we're doing it right. But ascent-based support asks you to trade those external validators for something quieter and more sustainable: *trust in the relationship you're building*. (Breaux & Smith, 2023)

When you stop measuring every interaction against an imagined finish line, you create space to notice what's actually happening. Your child's nervous system is learning that home is safe, that you won't demand more than they can offer, that their needs matter. Some days, maintaining routines will feel monotonous. You'll wonder whether repeating the same morning sequence for the hundredth time is actually helping or just keeping you stuck.

That doubt is natural.

But here's what matters: consistency isn't stagnation. It's the scaffolding that allows your child's development to unfold at a pace their nervous system can integrate. You're not doing nothing—you're doing the hardest work, showing up without guarantees, trusting process over proof. When you catch yourself spiraling into worry about timelines or comparing your child to others, come back to this: *small, steady, reliable*. That's the rhythm that changes everything, even when it doesn't feel like enough.

Cultivating Emotional Resilience

Trust-based parenting doesn't ask you to abandon structure or stop guiding your child toward growth. It asks you to redefine what growth actually means. When your child learns that emotions don't need to be hidden, that their preferences matter, that safety doesn't depend on perfect behavior—that's progress. It just doesn't look like the checklists promised it would.

You've spent this chapter learning to prioritize safety over compliance, predictability over surprise, autonomy over control. These aren't abstract principles. They're daily choices: acknowledging the broken cracker instead of minimizing the meltdown, offering two breakfast options instead of deciding for them, pausing before filling every silence with instruction. Each choice signals to your child's nervous system that *this space is different*. This adult doesn't need you to be smaller, quieter, easier.

Some parents worry this approach lacks rigor, that without constant correction their child won't learn what the world expects. But here's the distinction worth holding onto: teaching your child to trust themselves isn't the same as avoiding challenge. It's creating the foundation that makes challenge bearable.

A child who knows their emotions won't overwhelm you can tolerate discomfort without shutting down entirely. A child who experiences consistent autonomy develops the flexibility to handle situations where choice isn't available. You're not lowering expectations. You're building the internal scaffolding that makes meeting expectations possible.

As we move forward, we'll explore how this foundation translates into specific developmental domains—communication, social connection, sensory regulation. Research published in 2024 shows that trust-based, trauma-informed practices like Trust-Based Relational Intervention (TBRI) lead to meaningful improvements in children's attachment security and overall mental health after just one year (Misevičė et al., 2024). Research published in 2024 shows that trust-based, trauma-informed practices like Trust-Based Relational Intervention (TBRI) lead to meaningful improvements in children's attachment security and overall mental health after just one year (Misevičė et al., 2024). You'll see how trust doesn't just improve your relationship; it accelerates the very skills traditional approaches have been chasing all along. The child who feels safe trying, failing, and trying again without shame outpaces the child performing for approval every time. Not because they're working harder, but because their nervous system isn't spending half its energy on survival.

That's where we're headed next.

4

READING THE EARLY SIGNS: RECOGNIZING DYSREGULATION BEFORE THE MELTDOWN

MASTERING INTUITIVE OBSERVATION: BECOMING AN ATTUNED PARENT

Cultivating Mindful Awareness

Most parents of autistic children can tell you exactly when things started to fall apart on a difficult day. The moment is seared into memory—usually the *meltdown* itself. The screaming in the grocery store. The flung plate at dinner. The inconsolable sobbing that seemed to come from nowhere.

But here's what many of us miss: those moments didn't actually come from nowhere.

Meltdowns have a history. They build slowly, through what clinical experts call the "rumble stage"—a buildup phase of subtle cues sent long before a breakdown occurs (Myles & Southwick, 2005). A slight change in breathing pattern. Fingers that start picking at a shirt seam. A gaze that shifts from focused to distant. These aren't random behaviors—they're early warning signs, quiet distress signals that say

"I'm struggling" long before the struggle becomes visible to everyone in a ten-foot radius. The problem isn't that our children fail to communicate. It's that we haven't yet learned their language.

Mindful awareness is the practice of paying attention, on purpose, to what's happening right now—not what happened five minutes ago or what might happen in five minutes. For parents, this means learning to observe our children with fresh eyes in each moment, setting aside assumptions about what they *should* be doing or feeling and simply noticing what *is*.

It sounds deceptively simple. It's actually one of the hardest skills you'll develop, because it requires you to slow down in a world that rarely permits slowness.

When you cultivate this kind of awareness, you start catching the subtle shifts. You notice that your daughter touches her ear three times before she usually needs a break from noise. You see that your son's shoulders creep upward when the room gets too bright. You recognize the micro-expression that means "I'm about to lose it" a full ten minutes before things escalate. This isn't about hypervigilance or constant monitoring—it's about presence. Being there, really there, with your child. And that presence changes everything, because it gives you time.

Decoding Emotional Signals

Emotional signals are your child's primary communication system when words fail or haven't fully developed yet. They're the body's honest broadcast—faster than language, harder to suppress, and remarkably consistent once you learn the pattern. For autistic children especially, these signals often carry more reliable information than verbal communication, which can be effortful, delayed, or entirely inaccessible during moments of stress.

What does an emotional signal actually look like?

It's not always dramatic. A signal might be your son's sudden fascination with spinning the wheels on a toy car—something he does when overwhelmed, not when happily engaged. It could be your daughter's voice rising half an octave, a shift so subtle you'd miss it if you weren't listening closely. Maybe it's the way your child's eyes glaze over during a playdate, their body present but their engagement slowly retreating inward. These micro-shifts are the early warning system, the yellow light before the red.

Common emotional indicators that precede dysregulation include changes in breathing patterns—shallow, rapid breaths replacing the steady rhythm of calm. You might notice increased physical tension: shoulders hunching, fists clenching, jaw tightening. Some children become unusually quiet or withdraw from interaction, while others grow louder, more repetitive, or physically restless. Stimming behaviors often intensify or shift in quality, moving from soothing self-regulation to urgent discharge of mounting stress.

Learning to decode these cues means watching not just for individual signals, but for patterns. Does your child always fidget with their shirt collar before a meltdown? Do they stop making eye contact exactly three minutes before they need to leave the room? These patterns become your roadmap, allowing you to intervene with connection and support before dysregulation takes hold.

The goal isn't to prevent every difficult moment. It's to recognize the early signs so you can respond with understanding rather than react to crisis, fostering a home environment built on attunement instead of constant recovery.

Responding to Subtle Cues

When your child begins showing those early warning signs—the tensing shoulders, the faster breathing, the subtle withdrawal—what you do next either builds trust or erodes it.

Responsive attunement is the difference between a child who learns their nervous system can be understood and one who learns to hide their struggles until they explode. Research on parent-child attachment consistently shows that children develop emotional regulation not through isolation or independence, but through *co-regulation*—the experience of being met where they are, especially during distress. This matters profoundly for autistic children. When a parent recognizes dysregulation early and responds with compassion rather than correction, the child's brain receives a critical message: your signals are valid, your needs matter, and you are not alone in this. Over time, this repeated experience becomes the foundation for self-regulation, the internal capacity to manage overwhelming states. You can't rush a child into self-regulation; they have to feel regulation with you first.

The stakes are higher than most parents realize.

Children who repeatedly experience their distress signals being missed, dismissed, or met with frustration often stop signaling altogether. They learn to mask, to push through, to appear fine until they physically or emotionally can't anymore. This isn't resilience—it's nervous system shutdown. A landmark study in the journal *Autism in Adulthood* shows that suppressing these needs to appear neurotypical is a primary driver of autistic burnout, which leads to chronic exhaustion, loss of skills, and severe mental health struggles like anxiety and depression in adulthood (Raymaker et al., 2020).

What responsive support actually looks like varies by child, but the underlying principle remains constant: move toward, not away. When you notice your daughter's voice climbing higher, you might lower yours and slow your speech, offering your calm nervous system as a resource. When your son starts intensely fixating on that toy car, you might simply sit nearby, a quiet presence that says *I see you, I'm here*. Sometimes it's reducing demands—fewer questions, softer lighting, permission to step away. Other times it's providing sensory input they're seeking: a weighted lap pad, a chewy necklace, background music that drowns out unpredictable noise.

The goal isn't perfection. You'll miss signals. You'll misread them. What matters is the pattern you create over time—a consistent presence that says your child's internal experience is worth noticing, worth responding to, worth honoring.

DECODING BODY LANGUAGE: INTERPRETING NON-VERBAL CUES

Understanding the Language of Movement

Most autistic children communicate with their bodies long before they speak. When my daughter was four, she would rock on her heels before getting upset—a tiny motion I dismissed for months as restlessness. Once I saw the pattern, though, it was clear: heel rocking meant she was already working hard to stay regulated.

Body language functions as an emotional telegraph system. While neurotypical children might verbally express discomfort, many autistic kids bypass language entirely under stress, reverting to physical pathways. A stiff back isn't defiance; averted eyes aren't disrespect. These are active signals your child is sending you in real time.

The trouble is we're trained to read neurotypical body language, where eye contact signals engagement and stillness means cooperation. Autistic body language operates on different frequencies entirely. A child who goes motionless might be experiencing sensory shutdown, not calm. Indeed, a landmark study led by Steven Kapp confirmed that repetitive movements, or stimming, serve as crucial adaptive tools to soothe intense feelings and process sensory input (Kapp et al., 2019) (Kapp et al., 2019). The same behavior—like hand flapping—can express pure joy or acute distress depending on the moment. Context matters enormously.

Start with the extremities. Hands reveal tremendous information: are they relaxed, or curled into tight fists? Fluttering near the face versus slapping against thighs communicates entirely different nervous system states. Feet tell stories too—watch for toe-walking, which often intensifies under stress, or sudden stomping that signals overload building.

Shoulders creeping toward ears signal bracing, while a clenched jaw means the body is already in fight-or-flight, even if your child is sitting quietly. Posture shifts happen on a continuum. Your child might start a playdate upright, then gradually curl inward as stimulation accumulates—each incremental change broadcasting their internal state if you know how to listen with your eyes.

Identifying Key Non-Verbal Cues

Children speak volumes without saying a word. A hand that suddenly flutters near their face, shoulders that slowly creep toward their ears, eyes that dart toward the door—these small movements form a silent language that reveals everything about how your child is feeling in that moment.

Learning to read this body language transforms your ability to support your child before distress takes hold. When you notice your daughter's fingers beginning to tap rapidly against her leg during a family gathering, you're witnessing her nervous system sending an early warning signal. Her hands are telling you what her words cannot: the noise level is climbing past her comfort threshold, and she needs help before the overwhelm becomes unbearable.

Facial expressions offer another rich source of information, though they may look different than you expect. Some autistic children display subtle micro-expressions—a brief tightening around the eyes, a barely perceptible downturn of the mouth—that flash across their face before disappearing (Torres et al., 2025). Others might show delayed reactions, their expressions shifting several seconds after the triggering event (Oberman et al., 2009). Your child's face might remain remarkably still even as tension builds elsewhere in their body, or they might develop a fixed expression that serves as a protective mask.

Posture tells its own story. Notice how your child positions themselves in space. Do they lean away from certain stimuli? Curl inward when feeling vulnerable? Plant themselves firmly in doorways rather than entering rooms fully? These aren't random behaviors—they're purposeful responses to internal experiences you cannot see.

The key is recognizing your child's unique baseline. What does their body language look like when they're regulated and comfortable? Once you know their calm state intimately, deviations become visible. That slight change in breathing pattern, the new tension in their jaw, the shift from fluid movement to rigid stillness—these variations signal that something has changed internally, even if the external environment looks unchanged to you.

Start where you are. Pick one aspect of body language to observe closely this week. Watch their hands, or track their eye contact patterns, or notice their breathing. This focused attention builds your fluency in their non-verbal language, one gesture at a time.

Applying Non-Verbal Insights Daily

Build observation pauses directly into your existing routines. Before transitions—leaving for school, moving from dinner to bath time, heading out to the park—stop for five seconds and scan your child's body language. Are their shoulders tight? Is their breathing shallow? Have their hands begun repetitive movements? This brief checkpoint creates a habit of noticing before acting.

When you spot an early warning sign, name it internally without judgment. *"Her fingers are picking at her sleeve. That usually means the noise level is bothering her."* This mental noting separates observation from immediate reaction—a practice Jon and Myla Kabat-Zinn (1997) define as choosing to respond rather than react—giving you space to respond thoughtfully rather than reflexively (Kabat-Zinn & Kabat-Zinn, 1997).

Create a simple tracking system that works for your life, adapted from the Antecedent-Behavior-Consequence (ABC) model used in behavioral therapy. Some parents keep a notes app on their phone, jotting down what physical cues appeared before difficult moments. Others prefer a small notebook tucked in a kitchen drawer. Over one to two weeks, clear patterns emerge: your son's jaw clenches before grocery store meltdowns, your daughter's breathing speeds up twenty minutes into playdates, or foot-tapping intensifies during homework. These patterns become your early intervention roadmap.

Match your response to what you observe. If you notice increased stimming, ask yourself whether your child needs *more* sensory input to regulate or *less* environmental demand. Fidgeting hands might call for a chewy necklace or stress ball. Withdrawn posture might need reduced social pressure or a quiet space nearby. Your response doesn't need to be perfect—it needs to communicate that you're paying attention and trying to help.

Build response options collaboratively during calm moments. Show your child photos or videos of themselves displaying different body language—a technique known as video self-modeling (VSM)—and ask what they were feeling. Alternatively, utilize structured frameworks like The Zones of Regulation (Kuypers, 2011) to color-code physical and emotional states. This isn't always possible or productive, but when it works, it offers direct insight into their internal experience. Some children can't articulate feelings but can point to pictures representing "too loud" or "need break." (Kuypers, 2011)

The goal isn't controlling your child's body language or eliminating all signs of distress.

You're learning to read their communication system so you can offer support earlier, before their nervous system crosses into shutdown or meltdown. Every time you notice a cue and respond with attunement—even imperfectly—you're teaching your child that their internal experience matters and that regulation is possible with support.

EARLY INTERVENTION TECHNIQUES: ADDRESSING DYSREGULATION BEFORE IT ESCALATES

Understanding Triggers and Patterns

Start building your early intervention toolkit with a simple body-mapping exercise. Set aside fifteen minutes when your child is calm —perhaps during a favorite activity like drawing or watching a preferred show. Take photos or mental snapshots of what regulation looks like: hand position, facial expression, breathing rhythm, posture. Write down three physical details that signal "my child is comfortable right now." This becomes your reference point for everything that follows.

Next, identify one recurring challenging situation—maybe the transition from screen time to bedtime, or walking into noisy restaurants. For the next week, observe that specific situation three times. Don't intervene differently yet. Just watch and record what happens in your child's body five minutes before things escalate. You might notice their shoulders creeping toward their ears, fingers starting to fidget more rapidly, or their voice rising half an octave. These subtle shifts are your early warning system, the whispers before the storm.

Now comes the crucial part: pattern recognition. After documenting several instances, look for consistencies. Does your child always cover their ears in certain environments? Do they retreat to a corner when overwhelmed? Understanding these patterns allows you to anticipate needs rather than simply react to crises.

With this knowledge, you can begin crafting personalized interventions. If you notice your child tensing during transitions, introduce a five-minute warning with a visual timer (Dettmer et al., 2000). If loud environments trigger withdrawal, carry noise-canceling headphones (Pfeiffer et al., 2019) or plan shorter visits. The goal isn't to eliminate all discomfort—it's to catch dysregulation early enough that your child can still access their own coping strategies with your gentle support.

Remember, this detective work takes time. You're learning to read a language that has no direct translation, building fluency through patient observation and genuine curiosity about your child's inner experience.

Implementing Sensory Regulation Tools

Once you've identified your child's early warning signals, the next step involves assembling tools that actually work—not theoretical solutions, but concrete objects and strategies matched to your child's specific sensory profile. Build a sensory regulation kit as a collaborative project during a calm moment, letting your child touch and explore options rather than deciding for them what should be soothing.

Start with tactile tools. Some children need resistive input—therapy putty, stress balls, or chewable jewelry that provides oral stimulation *(Wilbarger & Wilbarger, 2002)*. Others require softer textures: silicone fidgets, smooth river stones, or fabric swatches with varying surfaces. Pay attention to what your child naturally gravitates toward when anxious. Do they pick at their sleeves? Consider a textured bracelet. Do they bite their shirt collars? A chewy necklace might redirect that need safely.

Auditory regulation matters enormously for children sensitive to sound.

Noise-canceling headphones aren't about withdrawal—they're about creating manageable sensory input so your child can remain present rather than fleeing entirely. Some families keep multiple pairs strategically placed: one in the car, one in the backpack, one near the dinner table. Loop earplugs offer a middle option, reducing volume without complete isolation, allowing your child to stay engaged while protecting their nervous system from overwhelm.

Visual supports deserve their own category. Many autistic children process visual information more reliably than verbal instructions, especially under stress. A laminated feelings chart small enough to fit in a pocket allows nonverbal communication when words fail. Visual timers transform abstract time into something concrete and manageable. Even a simple red/green card system—where your child can flash red to signal "I need space"—provides agency without requiring speech.

Proprioceptive input tools help children locate their bodies in space when dysregulation makes everything feel disconnected. Weighted lap pads (typically 5–10% of body weight), compression vests, or even a heavy backpack worn briefly can provide grounding deep pressure. Some children respond beautifully to resistance bands looped around chair legs, offering constant subtle input during seated activities.

The kit itself should live somewhere accessible—a designated basket, a specific backpack section, a drawer your child can reach independently. Accessibility determines whether tools actually get used when regulation starts slipping. During those five-minute observation pauses before transitions, you might ask, "Want to grab something from your kit before we go?" This gentle prompt builds the habit of proactive self-regulation. Rotate items periodically. What works brilliantly for three months might lose effectiveness as your child's nervous system habituates or their developmental needs shift.

Building Predictable Routines

Children feel most secure when the world around them follows patterns they can anticipate. For autistic children, who often process sensory input more intensely and may struggle with transitions, the predictability of daily routines becomes a powerful anchor. When a child knows what to expect—when meals happen, what bedtime looks like, how transitions unfold—their nervous system can relax into a state of readiness rather than vigilance. This doesn't mean every moment must be rigidly scheduled, but rather that the rhythm of the day provides enough consistency to feel safe.

Begin with foundational routines that bookend the day: morning wake-up sequences and evening wind-down rituals. These moments, when carefully structured, set the tone for regulation throughout the day. A morning routine might include waking to the same gentle music, following the same order of tasks (bathroom, breakfast, getting dressed), and using visual schedules to outline what comes next. Evening routines could incorporate dimmed lighting, calming sensory activities like rocking or gentle massage, and the same sequence of hygiene tasks before bed.

The key is consistency without rigidity. While the structure remains predictable, there's room for the child's input and natural variations. Perhaps your child chooses between two breakfast options or picks which pajamas to wear. These small choices within the routine foster autonomy while maintaining the security of structure. When unexpected changes must occur, prepare your child as much as possible using visual aids or simple verbal explanations, acknowledging that flexibility itself can become part of the trusted pattern.

Watch how your child responds to these routines and adjust accordingly. Some children thrive with tightly structured schedules, while others need more breathing room between activities. The goal isn't perfection—it's creating a rhythm that supports your child's unique nervous system, reducing the daily accumulation of stress that can lead to dysregulation.

Strengthening Emotional Vocabulary

Two years ago, if someone had told me that teaching my daughter words like "fizzy" and "heavy" would transform our hardest mornings, I would have been skeptical. Yet expanding her emotional vocabulary became our most practical intervention—not because she suddenly articulated complex feelings in complete sentences, but because she gained tools to communicate internal experiences that previously lived only in her body.

Children rarely possess the language to describe the spectrum between "fine" and "meltdown." Autistic children face additional barriers: alexithymia, the difficulty identifying emotions, is common, affecting an estimated 50% of autistic individuals (Bird & Cook, 2013). Under stress, the gap between what they feel and what they can express often widens. Without words for "overwhelmed" or "frustrated," the body becomes the primary messenger, turning intervention into crisis management rather than gentle support. (Bird & Cook, 2013)

Start with sensory language rather than emotional labels. Words like "buzzy," "squeezy," or "loud inside" connect directly to physical sensations your child already experiences. During calm moments, introduce these terms through play. Squeeze a stuffed animal and say, "My body feels squeezy right now—tight and compressed," then offer the same sensation through a firm hug. Notice their physical signs and gently narrate: "I see your hands covering your ears—are sounds too loud?"

Games keep this learning playful rather than clinical. Use cards and let your child match facial expressions to situations. Create a "feelings chart" with simple colors representing different states. Many families use bodily sensation mapping—inspired by research on how emotions manifest physically (Nummenmaa et al., 2014)—where children color a body outline to show where they feel specific emotions.

Progress is rarely linear.

Some days your child will use this vocabulary fluently; other days, words disappear under stress. That isn't regression—it's simply how the nervous system functions. Focus on building a shared language slowly, celebrating when they use "wobbly" to describe anxiety or point to a "red zone" instead of hitting. Every communicative step is a major victory, even on days when progress feels hard to see.

5

CREATING DAILY RITUALS THAT SUPPORT REGULATION AND CONNECTION

ESTABLISHING CONNECTION-FOCUSED ROUTINES

Morning Rituals for Connection

When my son was four, I tried everything to make our mornings smoother. I printed visual schedules. I set out clothes the night before. I bought special incentive charts with colorful stickers. None of it worked. He'd wake up already dysregulated, and by the time we got to breakfast, we were both exhausted from the battle.

One morning, out of sheer desperation, I stopped trying to move him through the routine.

Instead, I sat on the floor beside his bed and just waited. He eventually crawled into my lap, still half-asleep, and we sat there together in the quiet. No schedule to meet. Just ten minutes of stillness before the day began. Everything changed.

Not instantly—I'm not going to tell you that one calm morning fixed everything. But that small shift, that decision to prioritize connection over productivity, became the foundation of a morning ritual that actually worked. Because here's what I learned: mornings aren't about getting your child ready for the day. They're about helping your child *feel* ready for the day. And those are two very different things.

When we think about morning routines, we often focus on logistics—brushing teeth, getting dressed, eating breakfast, heading out the door. But for many autistic children, mornings involve a nervous system that's just waking up, still vulnerable and unsteady (Makris et al., 2022). Rushing through tasks before that system is regulated is like asking someone to run a marathon before they've had their coffee. It's not about defiance or difficulty; it's about developmental readiness.

So how do we create morning rituals that support both regulation and connection? We start by building in what I call anchor moments—brief, predictable interactions that ground your child emotionally before the day's demands begin. For us, it became those ten minutes of quiet closeness. For you, it might be a gentle hand on their back, a favorite song played softly, or simply sitting together while they wake up at their own pace.

The key is consistency, not rigidity. Your child's nervous system craves predictability, but that doesn't mean every morning has to look identical. It means they can count on *you* being present, calm, and attuned to their needs. It means knowing that before anything is asked of them, they'll have a moment to simply be.

From there, you can layer in the practical tasks—but always with the relationship as the guide. Does your child need movement to regulate? Maybe breakfast happens after a few minutes of stretching or bouncing on a therapy ball. Do they need silence? Perhaps mornings are a screen-free, low-stimulation zone until they signal readiness for more interaction. The routine serves the child, not the other way around.

What I wish I'd known earlier is that connection isn't an extra step—it's the step that makes all the others possible (Ting & Weiss, 2017). When my son felt seen and safe first, he could handle getting dressed. When his nervous system was steady, brushing teeth didn't become a power struggle. The tasks didn't disappear, but the resistance did.

Your morning ritual doesn't need to be elaborate. It just needs to be yours—shaped by your child's rhythm, your family's needs, and the understanding that how your child *feels* at the start of the day matters more than how much you accomplish.

Playtime as a Bonding Tool

Play isn't separate from development. It's where development happens.

Most of us think of play as recreation—something our kids do to burn energy or stay entertained. But for autistic children, play is the primary language of connection. It's where they practice communication without the pressure of words, where they explore emotions in a context they control, and where relationship-building happens without forced eye contact or scripted social rules.

The challenge is that traditional play—especially the kind modeled in parenting books or preschool settings—often doesn't match how autistic children naturally engage. We're told to encourage turn-taking, pretend scenarios, and group activities.

But what if your child prefers lining up toys in precise patterns? What if they'd rather spin objects than stack them? What if their idea of play looks nothing like the developmental charts suggest it should?

This is where connection-focused play begins: by following your child's lead instead of redirecting it.

When you join your child in their world—whether that means organizing toy cars by color, repeating a favorite phrase in different silly voices, or simply sitting nearby while they engage in solitary sensory exploration—you're communicating something profound. You're saying: *I see you.*

I value what matters to you. I'm not here to change you.

Start by observing what genuinely lights your child up. Is it the texture of sand? The sound of a particular song?

The predictable motion of a spinning wheel? Once you identify these anchors of joy, you can gently weave yourself into their experience. Narrate what they're doing in a calm, descriptive tone. Offer a parallel activity that mirrors theirs.

Introduce small variations only when they seem open and regulated.

The goal isn't to steer play toward "appropriate" outcomes. The goal is to build trust, attunement, and shared enjoyment—the foundation for all future communication and emotional growth.

Bedtime Routines for Emotional Security

Bedtime routines collapse when parents treat them as checklists rather than emotional landing pads. Bath, teeth, book, lights out—it looks efficient on paper. But for an autistic child whose nervous system has been processing sensory input, navigating social demands, and managing unpredictability all day, a rushed sequence of transitions can feel like one final assault before sleep.

The stakes here aren't just about getting your child to bed on time. Poor sleep affects emotional regulation, learning capacity, physical health, and family functioning. Research consistently shows that 50% to 80% of autistic children experience sleep disturbances—including difficulties falling asleep, frequent night wakings, and early morning awakening—compared to only 9% to 50% of neurotypical peers (Reynolds & Malow, 2011). But here's what matters more: bedtime is often the last interaction you have with your child each day. If it ends in frustration, meltdowns, or disconnection, that emotional residue lingers for both of you. (Reynolds & Malow, 2011)

When bedtime becomes a battle, everyone suffers. You lose your evening recovery time. Your child goes to sleep dysregulated, which affects the quality of their rest. The next day starts from a deficit, and the cycle repeats.

Connection-focused bedtime routines flip the script entirely.

Instead of viewing bedtime as a series of tasks to complete, you design it as a *regulatory bridge*—a predictable, calming sequence that helps your child's nervous system downshift from the demands of the day. This means building in time for co-regulation, not just compliance. It means prioritizing what actually soothes your child, even if it doesn't match conventional sleep hygiene advice.

Maybe your child needs deep pressure before sleep—a weighted blanket, tight hugs, or even lying under couch cushions for a few minutes. Maybe they need the same story read in the same cadence every single night, not for the plot but for the predictable rhythm of your voice. Maybe they need to process their day through sensory play with kinetic sand or by organizing their collection of small objects one more time.

The routine itself becomes the container for safety.

When each step happens in the same order, announced with the same gentle cues, your child's brain can stop scanning for what comes next. They can actually begin to relax. And when you weave in moments of true connection—eye contact they initiate, a shared giggle, a quiet question about their day that you don't force them to answer—you're not just putting them to bed. You're sending them into sleep feeling seen, regulated, and secure.

INCORPORATING SENSORY BREAKS INTO DAILY LIFE

Understanding Sensory Needs

Autistic children experience the world through a nervous system that processes sensory information differently; in fact, research indicates that between 45% and 95% of autistic children experience atypical sensory modulation (Ben-Sasson et al., 2009). Textures feel sharper, sounds arrive louder, lights seem brighter, and movement can either soothe or overwhelm in ways neurotypical systems don't register.

This isn't about being "too sensitive"—it's about neurological wiring that processes sensory input with different thresholds, speeds, and intensities. When sensory input exceeds a child's capacity to integrate it, dysregulation follows—not as a behavioral choice, but as a physiological response.

Sensory breaks aren't rewards or luxuries. They're regulatory tools that allow an overwhelmed nervous system to recalibrate before reaching crisis. When we wait until meltdown to address sensory overload, we've missed the window where regulation is still accessible.

The challenge lies in recognizing early signs that a child needs support. These signals rarely arrive as clear requests. Instead, they appear as subtle shifts: increased stimming, withdrawing from interaction, heightened irritability, or seeking intense sensory input like crashing into furniture or pressing against walls. Some children become hyperactive, unable to settle. Others go quiet and still, their bodies shutting down input entirely. A child who suddenly covers their ears in a previously tolerable environment, or who starts humming loudly during dinner, isn't being difficult—they're attempting self-regulation with the tools available to them.

Without intervention, these early cues escalate.

The child who was fidgeting five minutes ago may now be unable to respond to their name. The one seeking pressure might start hitting or biting—not aggression, but desperate attempts to meet an urgent sensory need. By the time we see what looks like a behavioral problem, the nervous system has already moved past the point where simple sensory input can help. Prevention requires learning your child's unique early warning system and responding before dysregulation takes hold.

Sensory breaks create space for the nervous system to process and reset. For some children, this means movement: jumping on a trampoline, spinning, pushing heavy objects, or deep pressure from weighted blankets. For others, it's reduction: dimming lights, eliminating noise, retreating to a quiet corner with soft textures. Still others need oral input—chewing, sucking through straws, crunching specific foods. What matters isn't the specific activity but whether it matches your child's nervous system's current need.

Building sensory breaks into daily life means anticipating when regulation will be challenged. Transitions between activities, environments with unpredictable stimuli, and periods of sustained focus all deplete regulatory capacity. A child returning from school has spent hours managing sensory input in fluorescent-lit classrooms with unpredictable sounds and social demands. Expecting immediate conversation or homework without a sensory reset ignores what their body has endured.

When parents start offering proactive sensory breaks—ten minutes on the swing before dinner, a basket of textured objects available during transitions, permission to retreat to a dim room when overwhelmed—they often see what they previously labeled as defiance dissolve. The child wasn't refusing to cooperate. They were trying to survive in a body experiencing sensory assault. Sensory breaks don't eliminate challenges, but they prevent the cascade from discomfort into crisis, creating a foundation where connection and learning become possible.

Practical Implementation Strategies

Families who weave sensory breaks into daily routines experience something unexpected. Yes, meltdowns decrease—that's measurable, documented, significant (Dehghani et al., 2025). But the deeper shift happens in *where* and *when* dysregulation occurs. Before implementing sensory breaks, crisis moments pile up around predictable transitions: walking through the door after school, hearing "time for dinner," starting the bedtime routine.

After positioning sensory breaks strategically—right before these historical struggle points—children navigate transitions with lower physiological stress and fewer behavioral escalations. The families who see the most dramatic improvement don't scatter sensory activities randomly throughout the day. They place breaks deliberately, creating buffers exactly where their child needs them most.

Transitions drain your child's regulatory reserves faster than almost anything else.

Moving from one activity to another demands that the nervous system disengage from current sensory input, tolerate uncertainty, and prepare for new demands—all while processing whatever residual stimulation lingers from the previous environment. For autistic children, this neurological juggling act often exceeds available resources, especially when transitions happen abruptly or without warning. A sensory break positioned before the shift gives the nervous system what it needs to manage the change without cascading into overload.

Before leaving for school, offer five minutes of proprioceptive input: pushing against a wall, carrying a heavy backpack around the house, squeezing a resistance ball. Before dinner—when competing kitchen smells and sounds collide with your child's already-depleted regulation—provide a sensory reset. Time in a dim room with a weighted blanket. Jumping on a small trampoline. The break doesn't eliminate the transition, but it creates the internal space to handle it.

Mealtimes layer their own regulatory challenges. The sensory complexity of eating—textures, temperatures, smells, tastes, plus the social expectation of sitting still and engaging in conversation—can overwhelm children already operating near their threshold. Rather than pushing through meals that end in tears or refusal, incorporate sensory preparation beforehand and sensory supports during. Ten minutes before eating, offer calming or organizing input depending on your child's state. A sluggish child might need alerting activities like bouncing or crunching ice. An overstimulated one needs deep pressure or quiet movement like rocking.

During the meal itself, sensory tools become supports rather than distractions. A chewy necklace for oral input. A wobble cushion for movement needs. Fidget items that allow hands to stay busy while the child remains at the table. What looks like fidgeting is often the exact input that makes sitting possible.

Timing determines whether a sensory break prevents crisis or simply interrupts one. A child offered a sensory break after they're already dysregulated may not be able to engage with the input—their nervous system has shifted into fight-or-flight, where regulation tools become inaccessible. But the same child offered a break when early signs appear—slight fidgeting, voice getting louder, withdrawing from interaction—can use sensory input to avoid escalation entirely.

This requires observation more than intervention. Track when your child typically struggles. Notice the fifteen minutes before difficulty starts. That's your window. A sensory break placed there interrupts the pattern before it hardens into crisis.

Play naturally incorporates sensory regulation when we allow it to unfold. Children instinctively seek the input they need: the child who crashes into couch cushions craves proprioceptive feedback; the one spinning seeks vestibular input; the one lining up toys may be using visual organization to calm an overstimulated system. Rather than redirecting these behaviors toward "appropriate" play, recognize them as self-regulation and build breaks around what already works.

Create a sensory corner stocked with tools your child gravitates toward—resistance bands, textured fabrics, objects to manipulate, a small trampoline, noise-canceling headphones. Location matters: placing it in a low-traffic area signals it's a retreat space, not a social zone. Then build access into the rhythm of your day, not as earned privilege but as available support whenever regulation needs it. The goal isn't controlling when your child uses these tools. It's ensuring they're accessible exactly when the nervous system requires them.

ENHANCING COMMUNICATION THROUGH RITUALS

Rituals for Non-Verbal Connection

Most communication with autistic children happens through what you *do* together, not what you say. Before language enters the picture, before verbal processing catches up with the moment, your bodies are already in conversation. That exchange speaks loudest when it's not forced but woven naturally into the small, repeated patterns you already share.

Start with one routine you're already doing. Maybe it's morning breakfast, the walk to the car, or the post-bath wind-down. Don't invent something elaborate or add a new task to your day—work with what's already there. Within that routine, identify a single moment where you pause and offer eye contact. Not demanding it, but simply making it available. When you place the plate down, wait a beat. When you hand over shoes, meet their gaze for a moment if they lift their head.

If they don't, notice what their body does instead.

That noticing matters more than the eye contact itself. Watch where your child's attention naturally goes during the ritual. Do they glance at your hands? Track your movements from the corner of their eye?

Turn their body toward yours without looking up? Those are their communication channels, and they're already open. Your job is to honor what's already happening rather than impose what you think should happen. If your child watches your hands, exaggerate the gesture slightly—show the toothbrush before bringing it close, hold the cup at eye level for a half-second longer. You're not teaching; you're amplifying the conversation that's already underway.

Once you've identified their preferred channel, build a predictable gesture into the routine. A thumbs-up when the task finishes. A gentle hand squeeze before transitions. An open palm that signals "your turn." Keep it consistent across days. As highlighted by the clinical Autistic SPACE framework (Doherty et al., 2023), providing predictability and dedicated processing space is crucial; when the routine remains stable, it reduces cognitive load, allowing your child to attend to the relational layer underneath (Doherty et al., 2023).

Then wait for them to return it. This might take days or weeks. They might modify your gesture into something that works better for their body—a head tilt instead of a nod, a hand tap instead of a squeeze. Let them lead that adaptation. You've created the container; they'll shape the content.

The mistake most parents make is measuring success by whether the child *performs* the gesture back. But the real shift happens in their nervous system. As expert Dr. Barry Prizant emphasizes, consistency and predictability are foundational for emotional regulation and nervous system safety. The moment your child recognizes the pattern, anticipates your movement, or relaxes into the rhythm, they're co-regulating. That internal change—invisible and quiet—is the connection you're building. (Prizant, 2015)

The gestures are just scaffolding.

Structuring Predictable Communication

Rituals create something powerful: a quiet promise between you and your child. Not a promise of perfection or flawless interaction, but a predictable moment where they know exactly what to expect. When you greet your child the same way each morning—whether with a gentle song, a touch on the shoulder, or a simple "good morning" paired with eye contact—you're building a communication anchor.

These anchors matter because autistic children often navigate a world that feels unpredictable and overwhelming. A consistent ritual offers relief from that uncertainty. Your child begins to anticipate the interaction, which lowers their anxiety and opens the door to genuine connection. Over time, these predictable moments become safe spaces where communication can unfold naturally, without pressure or demand.

Start small. Choose one or two moments in your day—perhaps morning wake-up or bedtime—and commit to a simple, repeatable pattern. Maybe it's a visual check-in card you show each morning, asking "How are you feeling today?" Maybe it's a bedtime routine where you both share one thing from the day, using pictures or words. The method matters less than the consistency.

What you're really doing is teaching your child that communication has rhythm and safety.

The Hanen Centre's research on neurodivergent communication (Sussman, 2012) highlights how daily routines provide essential scaffolding for language development and emotional expression. When interactions follow a predictable structure, children can focus less on *what's happening next* and more on *how to respond*. That shift is everything.

Progress might look quiet. One morning, your child glances up during your greeting ritual. Another day, they initiate the goodbye wave you've practiced together for weeks. These aren't dramatic milestones, but they're real communication growth—rooted in trust, familiarity, and the steady presence you've created. The ritual doesn't force connection; it invites it, gently and repeatedly, until your child feels ready to step in.

Integrating Sensory-Friendly Communication

What ties all of this together—the rhythms you establish, the sensory awareness you develop, the small rituals you protect—is a single core insight: communication happens best when the body feels safe. You can't separate your child's nervous system from their ability to connect with you. When sensory input overwhelms, when environments assault rather than support, communication shuts down not because your child won't engage, but because they physiologically can't.

Sensory-friendly communication rituals aren't about adding complexity to your day. They're about removing the invisible barriers that make interaction exhausting for your child. A dimmed hallway for morning greetings. A weighted lap pad during your evening check-in. A chewy necklace available during dinner conversation. These aren't accommodations in the deficit sense—they're *access points* that let your child's true communication capacity emerge.

When you choose the right environment, your child's energy shifts from managing sensory assault to actually being present with you.

Some parents worry that relying on sensory supports means their child won't learn to cope with "normal" environments. But research and lived experience confirm that consistent sensory support helps children develop stronger regulatory skills. A scoping review on sensory adaptive environments by Williams et al. (2024) highlights how tailored auditory, visual, and tactile tools reduce distress and promote meaningful participation in everyday activities. Over time, children learn what their bodies need, recognize their own physiological signals earlier, and eventually advocate for themselves. You're not creating dependency—you're teaching self-awareness.

The beauty of building sensory elements into your rituals is how quickly the results show themselves. A classic study by Schilling and Schwartz (2004) demonstrated that simple adjustments like alternative dynamic seating—specifically therapy balls—improved in-seat behavior and legible word productivity in children with autism. The child who squirmed through every mealtime conversation suddenly sits engaged when offered a wobble cushion. The morning routine that once triggered shutdown becomes a moment of genuine connection when you add noise-canceling headphones during transitions. These aren't dramatic interventions requiring professional oversight—they're intuitive adjustments that honor how your child's body works.

Start by observing which sensory inputs calm your child and which agitate them. Does soft lighting help them settle? Does background music soothe or distract? Does having something to fidget with free up their attention for conversation, or does it pull focus away? There's no universal sensory profile—your child's needs are as unique as their fingerprint. The goal is to create communication rituals where the sensory environment supports rather than sabotages connection, where your child's nervous system can relax enough to let their voice through.

6

RESPONDING TO MELTDOWNS WITH COMPASSION INSTEAD OF CONTROL

UNDERSTANDING THE ROOT CAUSES OF MELTDOWNS

Sensory Triggers and Overload

When my son was four, a trip to the grocery store reliably ended with him screaming on the floor. I tried warnings, countdowns, sticker charts, and consequences—nothing worked.

I thought he was being defiant. I worried I was failing as a parent. It wasn't until a particularly difficult afternoon that I noticed what I'd been missing all along: the fluorescent lights buzzing overhead, the relentless hum of industrial cooling units, the overwhelming clash of voices and shopping carts echoing through the aisles. My son wasn't misbehaving. He was drowning in sensory input that his nervous system couldn't filter or regulate.

For many autistic children, sensory triggers are the invisible currents pulling them toward dysregulation (Leekam et al., 2007). What seems like ordinary background noise to us can feel like standing next to a jet engine to them. A soft cotton shirt might scratch like sandpaper. The smell of cleaning products can be nauseating. These aren't preferences or pickiness—they're neurological realities that demand our attention and respect.

Understanding sensory processing means recognizing that your child's brain receives and interprets information differently. Some children are hypersensitive, overwhelmed by inputs that others barely notice—a pattern of sensory reactivity that is recognized as a key diagnostic feature of autism (American Psychiatric Association, 2013). Others are hyposensitive, constantly seeking more intense sensory experiences to feel regulated. Many children experience both, depending on the sense and the situation.

The path forward begins with observation. Watch for patterns: Does your child cover their ears in certain spaces? Do they avoid specific textures or seek out tight hugs? These behaviors aren't random—they're communication. Your child is showing you what their nervous system needs, even when they can't verbalize it.

Once you identify triggers, you can begin to modify environments—an approach supported by clinical evidence for improving child participation and reducing distress (Bodison & Parham, 2018)—and prepare your child for challenging situations. Noise-canceling headphones, sunglasses, a familiar comfort item, or simply leaving before overwhelm hits—these small adjustments honor your child's sensory reality and prevent meltdowns from igniting in the first place.

Emotional Underpinnings and Anxiety

Sensory overload ignites meltdowns from the outside in. But equally powerful—and often harder to detect—are the emotional currents that build from the inside out.

Anxiety doesn't always look like worry. In autistic children, it can appear as rigidity, explosive anger, or complete shutdown. Your child might insist on the same routine, plate, or route to school—not because they're being difficult, but because predictability is the only anchor they have in a chaotic world.

When that anchor slips, even slightly, the flood of emotion can be immediate and overwhelming.

Many autistic children experience what researchers call *alexithymia*—difficulty identifying and describing their own emotions. Studies show that about 50 percent of autistic individuals experience this condition, compared to roughly 5 to 10 percent of the general population (Kinnaird et al., 2019) (Kinnaird et al., 2019). They feel distress building inside but can't name it, locate its source, or communicate what they need. By the time you notice, they've already been sitting with mounting overwhelm for hours.

This is why asking "What's wrong?" during a meltdown rarely helps.

Emotional regulation is a learned skill, and autistic children often need more explicit teaching than their neurotypical peers. They may struggle to distinguish between frustration, disappointment, and fear, or fail to recognize early physical signs of escalating emotion—like tightness in the chest or heat in the face.

Without these internal cues, emotions arrive like sudden, uncontrollable storms.

Your role isn't to talk them out of feelings or distract them from discomfort. It's to create emotional safety by staying calm, predictable, and present. Name what you observe without judgment: "Your body looks tense" or "I'm here with you." Model slow breathing. Offer gentle reassurance that the feeling will pass. You're not fixing the emotion—you're teaching your child that emotions can be *felt* and *survived*, and that they don't have to face them alone.

Disrupted routines don't just annoy autistic children—they can dismantle their sense of safety entirely. When the morning unfolds in an unexpected order, or when a familiar route is suddenly blocked, your child isn't being inflexible. They're responding to what feels like the ground shifting beneath them.

Predictability creates cognitive breathing room. Neurotypical children can adapt on the fly because their brains automatically filter what matters from what doesn't. But for many autistic children, *everything* carries equal weight. The sequence of breakfast, the placement of shoes, the exact timing of departure—these aren't preferences. They're the scaffolding holding an overwhelming world in place.

When that scaffolding collapses without warning, the nervous system floods with cortisol. Research has shown that elevated levels of this stress hormone in autistic children are directly tied to daily stress caused by changes in routine (Corbett et al., 2009). The meltdown that follows isn't manipulation—it's a physiological response to perceived threat.

Transitions are particularly treacherous. Your child might be fine reading a book, and fine eating lunch, but the shift *between* those states requires mental flexibility that's often in short supply. Without preparation, transitions feel like being yanked from calm into chaos.

This is why advance notice matters so deeply. A five-minute warning before leaving the park isn't about obedience—it's about giving your child's brain time to disengage from the present and prepare for what comes next. Visual schedules, timers, and consistent language all serve the same function: reducing the cognitive load of constant uncertainty.

You can't eliminate all unpredictability. Life happens. But you can distinguish between necessary changes and unnecessary ones. Ask yourself: does this disruption serve my child, or does it serve my convenience? Sometimes the answer is both, and that's okay—but knowing the difference helps you prepare accordingly, offering the extra support your child needs when change becomes unavoidable.

STRATEGIES FOR MAINTAINING CALM DURING ESCALATION

Grounding Techniques for Parents

When your child is escalating, your nervous system often mirrors theirs—a biological and behavioral synchrony known as co-regulation

(Bornstein & Esposito, 2023). Your heart races, your muscles tense, your breath quickens. This physiological response is natural—it's your body preparing to protect. But here's the paradox: the calmer you remain, the safer your child feels, and the faster they can begin to regulate.

Deep breathing isn't just a cliché—it's a biological reset button. When you feel the first surge of panic as your child begins to dysregulate, place one hand on your chest and one on your belly. Breathe in slowly through your nose for a count of four, hold for four, and exhale through your mouth for six. This simple act activates your parasympathetic nervous system through respiratory vagal nerve stimulation, signaling to your body that you're safe (Gerritsen & Band, 2018). More importantly, it signals to your child that *they're* safe with you.

Visualization offers another powerful anchor. Picture yourself as a sturdy tree in a storm—your child's distress is the wind, powerful and unpredictable, but you remain rooted. Your branches may sway, but your trunk holds firm. This mental image reminds you that their emotional weather isn't yours to absorb; it's yours to witness with compassion.

Mindful pauses create space between reaction and response. Before you speak or move toward your child, take three seconds. Count them silently. This brief pause prevents you from adding your own dysregulation to theirs. It transforms "What do I need to fix?" into "What does my child need right now?"

Your body language communicates volumes during these moments. Soften your facial expression, even if your child isn't making eye contact. Lower your shoulders. Unclench your jaw. Keep your hands visible and open, never reaching or grabbing. Kneel to their level if safe to do so. These small adjustments telegraph safety without words, creating the conditions for de-escalation to begin naturally.

Some parents find it helpful to develop a personal mantra—a simple phrase that grounds them when chaos erupts. "This will pass." "I am their anchor." "Connection over correction" (Kennedy, 2022).

Repeat it silently as you breathe, letting it steady your thoughts the way your presence steadies your child.

Your calm isn't about suppressing your own feelings or pretending you're not affected. It's about choosing, in that critical moment, to prioritize regulation over reaction.

That steadiness begins with you.

Creating a Safe Emotional Space

Research from Yale University demonstrates what many parents discover through painful trial and error: the *manner* in which you respond during a meltdown matters as much as any specific intervention (Gee & Cohodes, 2021) (Gee & Cohodes, 2021). When developmental neuroscientists analyzed caregiver-child interactions during times of distress, they established that predictable parent responses and clear safety cues serve as crucial external regulators for an overwhelmed child, helping to stabilize their immediate nervous system response and strengthen the neural pathways responsible for long-term emotion regulation.

Consider Maya, a seven-year-old who experienced frequent meltdowns at school transitions. Her mother, Rachel, initially responded with rapid-fire questions and physical comfort attempts. "What happened? Are you okay? Let me help you!" she'd say, reaching out to touch Maya's shoulder while her voice climbed higher with each word.

Maya's meltdowns only intensified. The well-meaning questions felt like demands Maya couldn't answer. The touch overwhelmed her already overloaded sensory system. Rachel's rising anxiety became another stressor in an already chaotic moment.

Everything shifted when Rachel learned to create what I call quiet presence.

Instead of rushing in with words and touch, Rachel began positioning herself at Maya's eye level but slightly to the side, avoiding direct eye contact that could feel confrontational. She lowered her voice to barely above a whisper, sometimes saying nothing at all for the first minute or two. Her body language communicated one simple message: *I'm here. You're safe. Take your time.* This wasn't passive witnessing. Rachel remained fully present and attentive, ready to respond if Maya needed her, but she stopped trying to fix or stop the meltdown. She stopped treating the emotional storm as an emergency requiring immediate intervention.

The change was remarkable. Maya's meltdowns didn't disappear, but they became shorter and less intense. More importantly, Maya began seeking Rachel out *before* reaching the point of complete overwhelm, because she'd learned that her mother's presence meant safety rather than additional sensory or emotional demands.

Creating an emotionally safe space during escalation involves three core elements: reducing sensory input, communicating safety through body language, and maintaining your own regulation. Think of yourself as a calm anchor in your child's emotional storm. Your nervous system literally influences theirs through a process called co-regulation, where your child's dysregulated state can begin to synchronize with your regulated presence (Bornstein & Esposito, 2023).

Start by lowering environmental stimulation wherever possible. Dim lights if you can. Reduce background noise. Create physical space. If your child is in a public place and can be safely moved, guide them to a quieter area. If moving isn't possible, position yourself between your child and the most overwhelming stimuli, using your body as a gentle buffer.

Your words during this time should be minimal, slow, and predictable. Some parents develop a simple phrase they repeat: "I'm here with you. You're safe." Others remain completely silent, trusting that their presence communicates what their child needs to know. The key is consistency. Your child's overwhelmed brain can't process complex language, but it can recognize familiar patterns that signal safety.

Watch your body language with the same attention you'd give to a precise dance. Keep your posture open and non-threatening. Soften your facial expression. Slow your breathing deliberately, making your exhales slightly longer than your inhales. This isn't just calming for you—your child will unconsciously register these physical cues of safety, even when they can't make eye contact or seem completely unaware of your presence.

Most crucially, tend to your own regulation. I know this feels nearly impossible when your child is in distress, when other people might be watching, when you're running late, when you feel scared or frustrated or helpless. But your regulation is perhaps the most powerful tool you have in this moment. Take those deep breaths I mentioned—not as a technique for your child, but as genuine self-care. Ground yourself by noticing physical sensations: your feet on the floor, your back against the wall, the temperature of the air. Remind yourself that this moment, as difficult as it is, will pass.

Your child is not broken. You are not failing. This is hard, and you're doing the best you can.

This is the work of building trust during the hardest moments, transforming crisis into connection.

REBUILDING CONNECTION AFTER A MELTDOWN

Validating Emotional Experiences

Start with the simplest practice: naming what you see. After the storm has passed and your child's breathing has steadied, you might say quietly, "That was really hard for you." Not a question. Not a probe. Just acknowledgment.

This isn't about extracting explanations or teaching lessons while emotions are still raw. Wait until your child has genuinely returned to baseline—maybe thirty minutes later, maybe the next morning. Then offer a simple reflection: "Earlier, when you threw the blocks, your whole body looked really frustrated." You're not adding judgment or asking them to apologize. You're simply *witnessing* what happened.

When you name emotions without layering on shame, you give your child permission to feel without fear (Siegel & Bryson, 2011). You're essentially saying, "What you experienced was real, and it matters." This validation becomes the bridge back to connection, letting your child know they're still safe with you, still understood, even after the hardest moments. Over time, this practice teaches them that all feelings are acceptable, even the overwhelming ones, and that you're a steady presence they can trust to stay calm when their world feels chaotic.

Some children might not respond verbally, and that's okay. A nod, a slight relaxation in their shoulders, or simply staying near you can signal that your words landed. The goal isn't a conversation—it's emotional attunement, showing up consistently with empathy rather than correction (Siegel & Hartzell, 2003). This quiet witnessing builds the foundation for deeper trust and, eventually, the ability to articulate feelings before they escalate.

Re-establishing Safety and Calm

Once the immediate crisis has passed and you've both steadied your breathing, certain actions help restore emotional safety more reliably than others.

Step one: reduce remaining stimulation. If the television's still on, turn it off. If fluorescent lights are buzzing overhead, switch to softer lighting or natural light from a window. If siblings are hovering nearby with questions, gently redirect them to another room. Your child's nervous system is still fragile, still recovering. Even neutral sensory input can feel overwhelming during this vulnerable window. Think of it like turning down the volume on everything except your presence.

Step two: offer physical comfort only if your child initiates or welcomes it. Some children crave a hug immediately after a meltdown; others need space to fully decompress before any touch feels safe. Watch for cues—do they lean toward you, or turn away? Do they reach for your hand, or pull their body inward? Respect what their body is telling you. You might quietly offer, "Would a hug help?" and honor whatever response comes, even if it's silence or a head shake.

For children who find deep pressure calming, a weighted blanket or firm squeeze can help their nervous system settle. For those who need movement, a gentle walk outside or rocking together might work better.

There's no universal script here, which can feel frustrating when you want clear answers. But this is where your knowledge of your specific child becomes the guide.

Step three: reestablish predictability. Once your child shows signs of genuine calm—steady breathing, softer body language, maybe even eye contact—briefly acknowledge what comes next. "We're going to have a snack in a few minutes," or "I'm going to sit right here with you." These aren't commands or consequences; they're *anchors*. Predictability signals safety to an overwhelmed brain, reassuring your child that the world has returned to a manageable rhythm (Perry & Szalavitz, 2006). They need to know what's coming, that chaos won't continue indefinitely.

What you're building here isn't just recovery from one meltdown—it's a template your child's nervous system will recognize next time.

Engaging in Reflective Conversations

Some parents rush the repair conversation, sitting down with their child while stress hormones are still peaking. Physiologically, cortisol levels typically take 20 to 60 minutes to return to baseline after an acute stress trigger. Asking, "Can we talk about what happened?" too soon reads as a threat—another demand when they're barely recovering. Give it thirty minutes, sometimes an hour. (Cymbiotika, 2026)

You'll know they're ready when their body language opens: they initiate conversation, ask for a snack, or return to a previous activity.

Another common pitfall: leading with your own distress. "You really scared me back there," or "I didn't know what to do." While honest, these statements shift emotional labor onto your child, asking them to manage your feelings when they've just finished struggling with their own. Save those reflections for your partner, a friend, your therapist. Your child needs to hear that you're steady, not that they've destabilized you.

Some children shut down entirely when asked open-ended questions like "What were you feeling?" Their brains can't access or articulate internal states that clearly, especially so soon after overwhelm. If you get silence or "I don't know," don't push. Instead, offer observations: "I noticed your body got really tense when your brother touched your project." This gives them language without demanding they produce it themselves. Younger children or those with limited verbal skills benefit from simpler frameworks. You might say, "Your body was telling me something was really hard," and leave space for them to nod or add detail if they can.

Don't mistake silence for disengagement—many children process these conversations internally even when they can't respond outwardly.

If you realize mid-conversation that you've misread their readiness—maybe their jaw tightens again or they turn away—stop immediately. "I think we both need more time. I'll be in the kitchen when you're ready." This isn't failure; it's responsiveness. You're modeling that repair doesn't follow a rigid timeline.

When you do misstep—ask too soon, say the wrong thing, misinterpret their cues—recovery is straightforward. Acknowledge it simply: "I think I started talking before you were ready. Let's try again later." Your willingness to repair *your* mistakes teaches them that connection can survive rupture, that imperfect attempts still matter.

Strengthening the Parent-Child Bond

After the storm passes and calm returns, the real work of connection begins. This isn't about analyzing what went wrong or launching into a teaching moment while emotions are still raw. It's about gently rebuilding the bridge between you and your child, brick by careful brick.

Start with presence, not words. Sit nearby without hovering. Let your child know through your body language—open posture, soft gaze, calm breathing—that you're available when they're ready. Some children need physical closeness immediately after a meltdown; others need space first, then gentle reentry into connection. Learning your child's specific pattern is more valuable than any generic protocol.

When they signal readiness—making eye contact, moving closer, initiating touch—meet them with warmth and acceptance. A simple "I'm here" or "You're safe now" reassures without demanding explanation or apology. This moment isn't about correcting behavior; it's about restoring trust.

Shared sensory experiences work beautifully here. Sitting together with a favorite blanket, listening to calming music, or engaging in a familiar sensory activity like playing with kinetic sand creates positive association without requiring verbal processing. These rituals become touchstones your child can count on: *No matter how big my feelings got, we always find our way back to each other.*

Later—maybe hours later, maybe the next day—you might have a brief, age-appropriate conversation about what happened. But even then, focus on understanding rather than correction. "I noticed things got really hard for you. What was happening?" gives your child language for their experience without shame or judgment.

The pattern you establish matters more than perfection in any single moment. Consistent repair teaches your child that disconnection isn't permanent, that relationships can weather storms and emerge stronger (Tronick & Gold, 2020). This knowledge becomes foundational to their emotional security and their capacity for healthy relationships throughout life.

7

BUILDING INTUITIVE CONNECTION THROUGH PRESENCE AND ATTUNEMENT

✦

THE POWER OF PRESENCE: WHY BEING TRULY PRESENT MATTERS

Understanding True Presence

My daughter once asked me to help her find a stuffed rabbit she'd misplaced. I was standing right next to her, phone in hand, scrolling through emails while saying "uh-huh" and "let me know if you need help." She asked three more times before finally sitting down on the floor and going silent.

I was there. But I wasn't *present*.

Presence isn't about proximity. It's about the quality of attention we bring to a moment. For autistic children, this distinction becomes even more pronounced. They're often processing sensory input, navigating social expectations, and managing internal experiences that we can't see. When we're physically near but mentally elsewhere, they feel it acutely.

True presence requires what psychiatrist and author Dr. Siegel calls *attunement*—a state of emotional resonance where you are not just observing your child but actively tuning into their internal world so they can "feel felt" (Siegel & Bryson, 2011). You notice the slight shift in their breathing before a meltdown begins. You catch the flicker of excitement when they line up their trains in a new pattern. You sense the frustration building when words won't come.

This kind of engagement can't happen when part of your mind is making tomorrow's grocery list or replaying an argument from earlier.

The challenge is that modern parenting often rewards multi-tasking efficiency over singular focus. We've been conditioned to believe that doing three things at once makes us better caregivers. But for children who already struggle to feel understood, our divided attention reinforces their sense of disconnection. They learn that even when we're looking directly at them, we might not truly see what they're trying to communicate.

Practical Ways to Be Present

Presence is a practice, not a personality trait. You don't need to be naturally calm or innately patient. You need to create conditions that make focused attention possible.

Some parents assume presence means meditating for an hour or achieving some zen-like state before interacting with their child. That's not what we're talking about. Presence can happen in thirty seconds if you prepare your nervous system and clear your mental clutter first. Before you walk into your child's room or sit down for breakfast together, pause. Take three slow breaths. Notice where you're holding tension in your body and consciously release it. This brief reset signals to your brain that you're shifting modes.

The second practice involves what pediatric psychologist Roger Harrison and other experts call "special time"—a daily ritual of child-led play that has been shown to reduce behavior problems and strengthen the parent-child bond. Just five to ten minutes of this focused attention matters more than two hours of half-present supervision (Harlan & Thomad, 2022).

During these windows, resist the urge to direct, teach, or correct.

Your role is simply to be available and responsive. If your child wants to build a simple block tower, sit nearby and imitate their actions without offering commands or instructions. The point of this playtime isn't skill-building or teaching rules—it is creating a predictable, secure space where connection can happen naturally. Based on the clinical principles of Parent-Child Interaction Therapy (PCIT), this non-judgmental presence helps build relational capital. On some days, a child might play independently while you watch with warm enthusiasm. On other days, they will gradually initiate closer contact, sharing their inner world with you.

Over time, the consistency of your unhurried focus becomes the ultimate foundation for deeper trust. These practices don't require special training or perfect execution. They require only your willingness to stop fragmenting your attention and offer your child something increasingly rare: the experience of being someone's complete focus.

Most parents already know what they should be doing. They've read the advice, attended the workshops, absorbed the expert recommendations. But knowing and doing are separated by an invisible force field of stress, exhaustion, and the relentless demands of modern life.

The barrier isn't understanding—it's bandwidth.

When your nervous system is chronically activated, presence becomes neurologically difficult. A 2019 study published in *Scientific Reports* found that parenting stress directly undermines mother-child attunement at a brain-to-brain level, weakening neural synchrony in the prefrontal cortex—the region responsible for empathy, emotional regulation, and understanding another's point of view (Azhari et al., 2019). When you are overwhelmed, this critical area of your brain goes offline. You are not choosing distraction; your biology is forcing it.

Technology compounds this problem in ways we're only beginning to measure. On average, parents check their smartphones dozens of times daily, with objective tracking studies showing an average of 67 pickups per day (Yuan et al., 2019). Each glance fragments attention, creating what researchers call "continuous partial attention"—a state where you're never fully anywhere.

Your child notices.

When a parent's gaze shifts to a screen, children often perceive this "technoference" immediately, escalating their behavior to recapture focus. Multitasking presents another stubborn obstacle. You tell yourself you can listen while folding laundry, respond while cooking dinner, connect while mentally reviewing tomorrow's schedule. But human brains don't actually multitask—they rapidly switch between tasks, and each switch costs cognitive energy and relational depth. When your child shares something meaningful and you're simultaneously planning the grocery list, they experience your physical presence but your emotional absence.

The cost of these barriers accumulates quietly. Children don't complain that you're distracted; they simply stop reaching for connection. They learn to save their important thoughts for never, to assume your attention isn't truly available. The relationship doesn't break dramatically—it erodes, one fragmented moment at a time, until you wonder why your child seems so distant.

~

PRACTICES FOR DEEPENING ATTUNEMENT AND CONNECTION

Mindful Listening Techniques

Mindful listening operates differently than ordinary hearing. Most adults listen while simultaneously planning responses, filtering input through assumptions, or waiting for pauses to insert their own agenda. Autistic children detect this divided attention instantly. Their communication—whether verbal, gestural, or behavioral—deserves reception without interference, interpretation, or immediate problem-solving.

The practice begins with clearing internal noise. Before engaging, notice your mental chatter: the to-do lists, the worries about tomorrow's appointment, the replay of this morning's argument. Acknowledge these thoughts, then deliberately set them aside. This creates space for genuine reception.

Focused attention means tracking multiple channels simultaneously. Watch your child's hands, which often communicate what words cannot. Notice the tension in their shoulders, the rhythm of their breathing, the direction of their gaze. Listen not just to their words, but to the pauses between them, the shifts in tone, the moments of silence that carry their own meaning.

Reflective responses demonstrate you're truly receiving what your child communicates. Instead of immediately offering solutions or redirecting behavior, mirror back what you observe: "I see your hands moving quickly" or "Your voice sounds different right now." This simple acknowledgment validates their experience without judgment or agenda.

Your body language speaks as loudly as your child's. Position yourself at their eye level. Soften your facial expression. Uncross your arms. Let your posture communicate openness and safety rather than evaluation or urgency. These physical adjustments create an environment where authentic communication can emerge, strengthening the trust that underlies all meaningful connection.

Emotionally Responsive Play

When my daughter was six, she spent three consecutive afternoons lining up wooden blocks in patterns I couldn't decipher. Not building, just arranging. My instinct was to redirect her toward "productive" play—maybe construct a tower, engage her in pretend scenarios. Instead, I sat down beside her and picked up a block.

I didn't speak. I simply placed my block parallel to hers, matching the spacing she'd established. She glanced at me, then continued her pattern. After several minutes, she handed me a blue block—a specific blue block—and pointed to a gap in her arrangement. I'd been invited in.

That afternoon taught me more about play-based connection than any parenting manual. Real connection through play doesn't require elaborate setups or educational objectives. It starts with observation—watching how your child naturally engages with their world, then *joining them there* rather than pulling them toward your agenda. When you follow your child's lead, you're communicating something profound: their interests matter, their way of experiencing joy is valid, and you're willing to enter their world on their terms—an approach shown to promote longer-lasting child cooperation and socioemotional competence (Kochanska et al., 2013).

This approach transforms ordinary moments into opportunities for emotional attunement. Notice what captures your child's attention during free play. Do they gravitate toward sensory experiences—water, sand, textures? Do they create repetitive patterns or scenarios? These preferences aren't random; they reflect how your child processes emotions and regulates their nervous system. By participating without redirecting, you build trust while gaining insight into their internal landscape. (Stern, 1985)

Start small. Sit nearby during play without an agenda. Mirror their actions occasionally. Offer materials that complement what they're already doing rather than introducing entirely new activities. When you notice a shift in their emotional state—excitement, frustration, deep focus—acknowledge it simply: "You seem really proud of that" or "This part feels tricky." You're teaching them that their emotional experiences are seen and understood, creating the foundation for deeper connection that extends far beyond playtime.

Creating Safe Emotional Spaces

Emotional safety isn't about preventing difficult feelings—it's about creating conditions where those feelings can surface without fear of judgment or punishment. When your child knows their emotions won't be dismissed or corrected, trust deepens organically.

Most parents accidentally communicate the opposite. When a child melts down over a "small" thing—a broken cracker, a scratchy tag, a slight change in routine—our instinct is to minimize: "It's okay, it's not a big deal." We mean well. We're trying to soothe. But what the child hears is: *Your reaction is wrong. Your feelings don't match reality (Linehan, 1993).*

For autistic children, this disconnect compounds. Their sensory and emotional experiences are already intense, often overwhelming. When we signal that their internal reality is invalid, they learn to hide distress rather than express it—a process known as social camouflaging or masking, which is conceptualized as a form of self-invalidation (Bemmouna & Weiner, 2023). The meltdowns don't disappear; they just happen later, bigger, or turn inward as shame.

Building emotional safety requires consistency in three areas: predictability, non-reactivity, and validation. Predictability means creating routines around emotional expression—not rigid schedules, but reliable patterns where feelings are expected and welcomed. This might look like a quiet check-in after school, a bedtime chat where emotions are named without fixing them, or simply pausing before transitions to acknowledge what your child might be feeling. Non-reactivity means staying calm when emotions run high, signaling through your tone and body language that their distress won't destabilize you. Validation means reflecting their experience back to them: "That cracker breaking really upset you. I see how hard that was." This practice of parent-child emotional validation has been shown to significantly improve children's emotional awareness and help them regulate their distress (Lambie et al., 2020).

When these three elements align, your child learns that their emotions are safe with you. They begin to trust that expressing fear, frustration, or sadness won't cost them your approval or presence. That trust becomes the foundation for every conversation, every transition, every moment of growth moving forward.

Daily Reflection Practices

Taking a few minutes at the end of each day to reflect on your interactions with your child can transform your ability to stay attuned. This isn't about judgment or creating another task on your to-do list—it's about building gentle awareness that deepens your connection over time.

Daily reflection exercises help you notice patterns in your responses, celebrate moments of genuine connection, and identify areas where you might need more support or understanding. Start with something simple: before bed, jot down one moment from the day when you felt truly connected to your child. What were you both doing? What did you notice about their body language or emotional state? How did you respond?

Journaling prompts can guide this practice without making it overwhelming. Try asking yourself: *When did my child seem most regulated today? What sensory or emotional needs did I notice? How did I respond to signs of dysregulation, and what might I do differently tomorrow?* These questions aren't about perfection—they're about cultivating the habit of paying attention.

Mindfulness techniques can also support your reflection practice. After a challenging interaction, pause for a few deep breaths and notice your own emotional state without judgment. Did you feel frustrated, overwhelmed, or disconnected? Simply acknowledging these feelings helps you approach the next moment with more clarity and compassion.

Over time, this reflective practice becomes a quiet anchor in your parenting journey. You'll start recognizing subtle shifts in your child's needs before they escalate, and you'll respond from a place of calm understanding rather than reactivity. Continuous growth in attunement doesn't happen overnight—it unfolds through small, consistent practices that honor both your humanity and your child's unique way of experiencing the world.

~

CREATING MEANINGFUL SHARED EXPERIENCES

Integrating Presence into Play

Start with ten minutes. Not your whole day, not a grand restructuring of your life—just ten minutes of protected time when you're truly present with your child, phones silenced, mental to-do list acknowledged and set aside.

Choose a moment when your child is naturally engaged in something they already enjoy. This might be lining up toy cars, drawing repetitive patterns, or watching shadows move across the wall. Sit down nearby without an agenda. Don't guide, teach, or redirect. Simply observe what captures their attention and how their body moves through the activity.

After a few minutes of quiet observation, try *parallel play*—doing the same activity alongside them without taking over. If they're stacking blocks, stack your own. If they're running fingers along textured fabric, do the same with a different piece nearby. You're not mimicking to mock or distract; you're entering their sensory world on their terms.

Watch for invitations.

These rarely look like verbal requests. Your child might glance at you, pause to see what you do next, hand you an object, or shift their body slightly toward yours. When you notice these moments, respond simply and without fanfare. Accept the block they offer. Place your hand near theirs. Match their rhythm.

Practice reflective tracking by quietly naming what you notice without judgment or interpretation. "You're putting all the red ones together." (Landreth, 2012). "Your hands are moving really fast right now." "You keep going back to that blue car." These observations aren't tests or prompts—they're acknowledgments that you see them, that their actions have meaning worth noticing.

After your ten minutes, take two minutes to write down one specific detail: a gesture, a sound, a moment when something shifted between you. Don't analyze it. Just record the observation. Repeat this daily for a week, keeping the time boundary firm. You're building a new muscle—the capacity to be fully present without fixing, teaching, or improving. Connection emerges not from doing more, but from being genuinely available in small, consistent moments where your child's experience becomes the center of your shared attention.

Cultivating Creativity Together

Some weeks will feel effortless. You'll notice your child leaning into connection, offering more eye contact, lingering longer in shared moments. Other weeks you'll wonder if anything you're doing makes a difference at all.

This isn't failure—it's the actual rhythm of development. Progress doesn't move in straight lines, especially for children whose nervous systems need time to process new patterns of interaction. Neuroplasticity research confirms that meaningful change happens through repetition over time, not dramatic breakthroughs (Kolb & Gibb, 2011) (Kolb & Gibb, 2011). Your child might seem distant for days, then suddenly initiate connection in a way they never have before.

The key is creating low-pressure collaborative projects that honor your child's interests without forcing outcomes. If your child loves building with blocks, sit beside them and build your own structure. Narrate what you're doing without expecting a response. This parallel play creates proximity without demands, allowing your child to observe, absorb, and eventually engage when they feel ready (Parten, 1932). You're modeling creativity while respecting their pace.

Notice what captures their attention naturally. Does your child gravitate toward water play, arranging objects in lines, or sorting by color? These aren't random behaviors—they're windows into what soothes and engages their sensory system. When you join them in these interests rather than redirecting toward what you think they *should* enjoy, you're communicating something profound: I see you. Your way of experiencing the world matters.

Try introducing simple variations once they seem comfortable. If they're lining up toy cars, add a new color to the sequence. If they're painting, offer a different brush size. These gentle expansions build flexibility while preserving the safety of the familiar pattern. You're not disrupting their process—you're gently stretching it, showing that creativity can evolve without losing its core comfort.

The trust you build through these shared moments becomes the foundation for every other developmental milestone ahead.

Reflective Practices for Connection

When the laughter fades and the game ends, a quiet moment of reflection can turn an ordinary afternoon into something profound. Taking time to revisit what you and your child just experienced together—whether it was building a fort, painting side by side, or simply lying on the floor watching dust motes dance in the sunlight —deepens the emotional imprint of that moment (Fivush et al., 2006). This isn't about formal debriefing or turning everything into a teaching opportunity. It's about pausing to notice what happened between you.

Try asking gentle, open-ended questions that invite your child to share their perspective. "What was your favorite part?" or "Did you notice how we figured that out together?" These simple prompts encourage your child to reflect on their own experience, reinforcing their sense of agency and self-awareness (Reese et al., 2007). Even if they don't respond with words, their body language or facial expressions often reveal what mattered most to them. Your attentive presence during these moments communicates that their feelings and thoughts are valued.

Gratitude practices woven into these reflections can be especially powerful. Naming something specific you appreciated—"I loved how patient you were when we tried to stack those blocks"—models positive recognition without pressure or performance expectations. It shifts the focus from outcome to connection, celebrating the process rather than perfection.

Over time, these reflective rituals become anchors in your family's rhythm. They create space to honor your child's unique way of experiencing the world while reinforcing the trust and safety that allow genuine connection to flourish. You're not just building memories; you're co-creating a narrative of shared joy, mutual respect, and emotional safety that supports every aspect of your child's growth. This is where developmental progress truly takes root—not in structured lessons, but in the fertile ground of felt connection.

8

SPEAKING YOUR CHILD'S LANGUAGE: COMMUNICATION STRATEGIES THAT WORK

✦

UNDERSTANDING YOUR CHILD'S UNIQUE COMMUNICATION STYLE

Identifying Communication Patterns

When my son was three, he used to line up his toy cars in precise, color-coded rows every single evening before bed. If I moved one—even slightly—he'd notice immediately and place it back exactly where it belonged. Other parents might have seen this as rigidity or a need for control. I saw something different.

This wasn't obstinance or lack of social interest. It was my son showing us what made sense to him, what brought order to an overwhelming sensory world, what he needed us to understand about how he processed information. Those carefully arranged cars were his way of saying, *"This is how I communicate calm. This is how I tell you I'm okay."*

Every child with autism develops their own unique communication style—a personal language built from gestures, routines, repetitive behaviors, tone shifts, and yes, sometimes words. But these patterns often look nothing like the communication scripts we expect. They require us to become fluent in a language we've never been taught.

Recognizing your child's communication patterns starts with observation without judgment. Watch how your child responds to different sensory inputs throughout the day. Does she hum when she's content? Does he retreat to a quiet corner when overwhelmed? Does she flap her hands when excited? These aren't behaviors to extinguish—they're vital pieces of her communicative repertoire (Kapp et al., 2019).

Pay attention to the context surrounding these patterns. Notice what happens right before your child covers their ears or starts scripting lines from a favorite show. These moments aren't random—they're purposeful responses to internal or external stimuli, and they're telling you something important about what your child needs in that moment.

Your child is always communicating. The question isn't whether they're speaking—it's whether we're listening in the right language.

Recognizing Strengths in Communication

Most parents I work with arrive exhausted from trying to fix what they perceive as broken. They've invested months—sometimes years—cataloging deficits, tracking delays, measuring gaps between their child and developmental milestones (Steiner, 2011). When I ask them to list their child's communication strengths, they often pause. The question catches them off guard.

Communication strength means any method your child uses effectively to express needs, preferences, emotions, or connection—regardless of whether it matches typical developmental expectations. It's not about whether your child uses full sentences or makes eye contact. It's about what actually works for them to convey meaning and be understood.

My daughter doesn't ask for help with words when she's frustrated with a puzzle. Instead, she brings me the piece, places it in my palm, and guides my hand toward the empty space. That's not a deficit. That's brilliant problem-solving wrapped in trust.

When you shift your lens from what's missing to what's present, everything changes. You begin noticing the way your child hums a specific tune when content, or how they arrange objects in precise patterns to communicate their need for order and predictability. You see the tap on your arm—not as an interruption, but as an invitation. These aren't behaviors to extinguish or redirect. They're functional communication that deserves recognition and respect.

Celebrating these strengths does more than validate your child's efforts. It fundamentally alters their willingness to engage. Children who feel understood—whose communication attempts are met with recognition rather than correction—naturally expand their repertoire (Siller & Sigman, 2002). They experiment more freely because the risk of failure diminishes when success is defined by connection rather than conformity.

Start by documenting three communication strengths this week. Not what you wish your child could do, but what they *already do* effectively. Maybe they use gestures with remarkable clarity, or perhaps they've developed a personalized sign system that family members intuitively understand. Write these down. Share them with anyone involved in your child's care. When you name these strengths aloud—*"You showed me exactly what you needed"*—you're not just acknowledging communication. You're building the trust that makes all future progress possible.

Building a Two-Way Understanding

When your child's communication attempt goes unrecognized, something shifts in their nervous system. Cortisol levels rise as physiological stress increases, and trust erodes incrementally. They try again—maybe louder, maybe through behavior you'll later call *dysregulation*. But from their perspective, they've been speaking clearly. You just weren't listening in their language.

Two-way understanding means both parties feel genuinely heard, not just that information successfully transfers from one person to another. It requires parents to adjust their receiving mechanisms as much as children adjust their sending ones. Most communication breakdowns happen not because autistic children can't communicate, but because we're waiting for communication that sounds like ours.

You might watch your child spend fifteen minutes arranging magnetic letters on the refrigerator while you cook dinner, barely glancing over and assuming they are simply playing. They grow increasingly agitated, finally sweeping all the letters onto the floor. Only when you actually look do you realize they've spelled "MILK" using the only letters they could reach. They've been asking for something specific, but you were too busy listening for spoken words to hear what they were actually saying.

Research on parent-child communication in autism consistently shows that parental responsiveness to a child's *existing* communication forms—rather than insistence on conventional methods—predicts better developmental outcomes across domains (Siller & Sigman, 2008). Children whose parents respond to gesture, eye gaze, or unconventional vocalizations with the same attentiveness given to speech develop stronger overall communication skills. The validation itself becomes scaffolding.

Reflective communication works by mirroring back what you understand before responding with your own agenda. When your child hands you their empty cup, you might say, "You want more water," and wait for confirmation—a nod, a reach, a sound—before filling it. You're checking your interpretation, not assuming it. This practice accomplishes something profound: it slows down exchanges enough that miscommunication becomes visible and repairable. It demonstrates that their perspective matters more than efficiency. And it teaches them, through repetition, that communication is collaborative—not a series of commands they either obey or resist.

Active listening with autistic children often requires releasing the expectation of eye contact, verbal responses, or immediate reactions.

Some children need processing time. Others communicate most clearly through their bodies or their play. When you narrate what you observe without demanding confirmation—*"You're lining up all the blue cars. You have a system"*—you're acknowledging their internal logic without requiring them to translate it into your preferred format.

The stakes here extend beyond individual moments. Children who experience consistent misunderstanding develop what researchers call learned helplessness in communication—they stop trying because the effort yields no meaningful response. But children whose attempts are met with genuine curiosity and reflection learn that their voice carries weight, that persistence brings connection, and that they possess something worth saying. That's the foundation every other communication skill builds upon.

~

HARNESSING THE POWER OF NON-VERBAL COMMUNICATION

Interpreting Non-Verbal Cues

Words precede understanding by years. Before any child says "I'm scared" or "That hurts," they've been speaking through the body—shoulders hunched, eyes averted, hands pressed over ears. For autistic children, this non-verbal language often remains their primary or preferred communication channel well beyond ages when peers transition to verbal explanations. Parents who learn to read these signals gain access to an ongoing conversation happening beneath what seems like silence.

Facial expressions carry enormous weight, yet they rarely arrive in the exaggerated forms parenting books describe. A slight furrow between the eyebrows might signal confusion. Lips pressed into a thin line often precede overwhelm, not defiance. When your daughter's eyes widen fractionally at the mention of the park, that's enthusiasm—even if she says nothing aloud. The challenge is that these expressions can be subtle, fleeting, and context-dependent. What looks like a blank stare might actually be intense concentration or sensory processing. What appears as a lack of reaction could be a delayed processing response—a phenomenon researchers have documented as a neurological lag in sensory and auditory processing (Bogdashina, 2003)—requiring several seconds or even up to a minute before a visible response. Parents accustomed to immediate, clear emotional displays sometimes miss the quieter vocabulary their child already uses fluently.

Body language operates as a complex signaling system, revealing emotional states often before the child consciously recognizes them.

A child who begins rocking gently isn't necessarily distressed. Rhythm frequently indicates self-regulation in progress, an attempt to maintain equilibrium amid competing sensory inputs. But when that same child's rocking accelerates, becomes more forceful, or pairs with other movements like hand-wringing, the body is broadcasting escalating stress. These patterns function like an early warning system, giving parents critical minutes to intervene with comfort or environmental adjustments before full dysregulation arrives. Similarly, a child who suddenly stiffens, pulls away from touch, or covers their face may be signaling sensory overload rather than rejection. The body knows what it needs before language can articulate it.

Hand movements tell their own stories. Flapping might express excitement, anxiety, or the need to release built-up energy—context determines meaning. Finger-tapping on surfaces could indicate thinking, self-soothing, or seeking tactile input. When your son repeatedly touches the same spot on the wall before entering a room, he's creating a sensory anchor, a predictable ritual that helps him transition between spaces. These aren't meaningless repetitions. They're purposeful communication about internal states and environmental needs.

Proximity and positioning reveal comfort levels with startling accuracy. The child who maintains three feet of distance during conversations isn't being standoffish—they're establishing the spatial boundary (Gessaroli et al., 2013) that allows them to process interaction without sensory overwhelm. The one who leans into your shoulder while you read together is communicating trust and contentment through physical closeness. Some children seek deep pressure when stressed, pressing themselves into couch cushions or requesting tight hugs. Others need space to breathe, literally and figuratively, creating distance to regain equilibrium. Both responses are valid, healthy forms of self-advocacy.

Learning to interpret these non-verbal cues requires slowing down and observing without judgment. Notice patterns across different situations. Does your child's posture change when transitioning from quiet play to group activities? Do certain facial expressions consistently appear before meltdowns? Keep a mental catalog of these signals, building a personalized dictionary of your child's non-verbal language. Over time, you'll recognize the difference between the hand-flapping that means "I'm thinking hard" and the hand-flapping that precedes sensory shutdown. You'll distinguish between the eye contact avoidance that indicates concentration and the kind that signals social anxiety.

The real transformation happens when you respond to these signals as legitimate communication rather than behaviors to correct. When your daughter covers her ears at the grocery store, that's not defiance—it's clear communication that the environment has exceeded her auditory threshold. Acknowledging the message by moving to a quieter area or offering noise-canceling headphones validates her self-advocacy and strengthens trust. When your son stiffens at an unexpected hug from a relative, he's communicating a boundary about touch. Protecting that boundary teaches him his body's messages matter and deserve respect.

This attunement to non-verbal communication doesn't just prevent meltdowns. It builds the foundation for all future communication development, verbal or otherwise. Children who feel understood through their body language develop confidence in their ability to be heard. That confidence encourages further communication attempts, creating an upward spiral of connection and trust that honors how they naturally express themselves.

Utilizing Non-Verbal Strategies

Research from Marion Rutherford and colleagues published in the *International Journal of Environmental Research and Public Health* provides remarkable validation for what many parents instinctively sense: incorporating visual supports in the home dramatically reduces daily difficulties for autistic children (Rutherford et al., 2023) (Rutherford et al., 2023). In their 2023 pilot study of 29 families, training parents to pair verbal directions with visual schedules, photo cards, or drawings led to statistically significant improvements in parent-reported quality of life and a noticeable reduction in autism-specific challenges. The implications reach far beyond academic settings.

When we intentionally harness non-verbal communication tools, we're not accommodating a deficit. We're matching our methods to how these children's brains naturally process information, honoring their unique wiring rather than forcing them to constantly translate our neurotypical approach.

Gestures become conversation partners. A simple thumbs-up when your child finishes a task, a gentle hand on the shoulder to signal transition time, or pointing to a visual schedule eliminates the ambiguity that spoken words sometimes carry. These physical cues ground abstract concepts in concrete, observable actions your child can see and internalize. When you pair "time to brush teeth" with a pointing gesture toward the bathroom and a toothbrush icon on the wall, you're creating multiple entry points for understanding—not because your child can't comprehend language, but because layered communication respects how their sensory system prioritizes visual and kinesthetic input.

Visual aids transform household chaos into predictable patterns. A morning routine chart with photos of each step—getting dressed, eating breakfast, packing the backpack—turns an overwhelming sequence into a manageable roadmap. Your child no longer has to hold multiple verbal instructions in working memory while simultaneously managing sensory input and emotional regulation. Instead, they glance at the chart, see what comes next, and move through their day with reduced anxiety and greater autonomy.

The beauty of this approach lies in its flexibility. Some children respond best to realistic photographs; others prefer simple line drawings or even abstract symbols they've helped create. One family I worked with discovered their daughter thrived when they used color-coded cards—green for preferred activities, yellow for transitions, red for challenging but necessary tasks. She began carrying her own set in a small pouch, pulling out the yellow card when she sensed a transition coming, essentially co-regulating with her parents through a shared visual language.

Body language speaks volumes when we learn to listen. Matching your child's energy level, getting down to their eye level during important conversations, and maintaining an open, relaxed posture signals safety and receptiveness. If your child is overwhelmed, your calm, grounded presence—demonstrated through slow movements and soft facial expressions—can be more regulating than any words you might offer. You're not performing these actions as manipulation tactics; you're genuinely attuning your non-verbal signals to create an environment where your child feels understood and safe enough to engage.

Start small. Choose one routine that consistently generates stress and introduce a single visual support or gestural cue. Notice what shifts. Does your child check the visual schedule unprompted? Do they mirror your calming gestures back to you during difficult moments? These small confirmations aren't just behavioral wins—they're evidence of deepening trust, proof that you're speaking a language your child's nervous system recognizes and responds to naturally.

~

CREATING EFFECTIVE SOCIAL STORIES AND VISUAL AIDS

Crafting Personalized Social Stories

Social stories work best when they meet your child in their current emotional state, not when anxiety is already building. Research by Gray & Garand (1993) and practical guidance from the National Autistic Society (2021) suggest introducing the narrative when your child is calm and relaxed. Monitor your child's optimal preparation window—introducing it too early can trigger anticipatory anxiety, while waiting until the day of the event might not allow sufficient time for them to absorb the information. (Gray & Garand, 1993)

Read the story together multiple times before the actual event. Research on the implementation of social stories (Ivey et al., 2004) suggests reviewing them daily for at least three to five days before the anticipated situation, allowing your child to internalize the sequence and expectations without pressure. Each reading reinforces familiarity, transforming the unknown into something manageable and less threatening.

During these readings, invite your child to participate actively. Ask gentle questions like, "What do you think happens next?" or "How do you feel about this part?" This engagement transforms passive listening into collaborative understanding, deepening their connection to the narrative and building confidence in their ability to navigate the upcoming experience.

After the event, revisit the story together as a reflection tool. Celebrate what went well and acknowledge any challenges without judgment. This post-event review reinforces the learning cycle, helping your child connect the story's framework to their lived experience. Over time, they'll develop an internal library of social scripts that reduce anxiety and increase their sense of competence in new situations.

Keep the story accessible. Place it somewhere your child can revisit independently—a shelf in their room, a digital device, or a special folder. Autonomy in accessing the story empowers them to self-regulate their anxiety, reinforcing the connection-first principle that your child is an active participant in their own growth, not a passive recipient of instruction.

As your child becomes familiar with the format, encourage them to help create future stories. Ask what details matter most to them, which pictures they'd like included, or how they'd describe certain feelings. This collaborative creation process honors their perspective, strengthens your intuitive connection, and ensures the stories remain truly personalized to their unique way of experiencing the world.

Utilizing Visual Aids for Clarity

Visual aids transform abstract concepts into concrete, tangible information that autistic children can process more easily (Meadan et al., 2011). When words feel slippery or overwhelming, a simple picture or symbol can anchor understanding and reduce anxiety (Rutherford et al., 2020). These tools aren't about dumbing things down—they're about speaking in a language your child's brain naturally understands.

Schedules are among the most powerful visual supports you can create. A daily schedule with pictures or icons showing the sequence of activities helps your child anticipate what's coming next, reducing the stress of unexpected transitions. You might use photos of actual locations in your home: the kitchen for breakfast, the bathroom for teeth-brushing, the car for school drop-off. Some children respond better to drawn symbols, while others prefer written words paired with images. The key is customization—what makes sense to your child's particular way of processing information.

Charts can clarify behavioral expectations without the need for lengthy verbal explanations. A simple feelings chart with faces showing different emotions gives your child a way to communicate their internal state when words fail them. A choice board displaying snack options or activity preferences empowers your child to express desires independently, building both communication skills and autonomy (Deel et al., 2021). These aren't compliance tools—they're bridges to mutual understanding.

Pictograms work beautifully for children who think in images rather than words. You might create a morning routine strip with small pictures showing each step: getting dressed, eating breakfast, brushing teeth, putting on shoes. Your child can move through the sequence at their own pace, checking off or removing each image as they complete it. This visual roadmap transforms an overwhelming series of demands into manageable, predictable steps.

The real magic happens when you involve your child in creating these aids. Let them choose the colors, pick the images, or even draw their own symbols. One parent discovered their daughter responded far better to hand-drawn stick figures than professional clipart—the homemade quality felt more personal and less institutional. Another family used photographs of their child actually doing each activity, which created immediate recognition and engagement.

Start simple and build gradually. You don't need to create an elaborate visual system overnight. Begin with one transition that consistently causes stress—maybe the shift from playtime to bedtime—and introduce a simple visual cue for that moment. A five-minute warning card showing a clock can prepare your child for an upcoming change. A transition object they carry from one activity to the next can provide continuity and comfort.

Remember that visual aids should evolve as your child grows. What works beautifully at age four might feel babyish at age seven. Stay attuned to your child's changing preferences and developmental stage, adjusting your visual supports accordingly. The goal is always clarity, autonomy, and reduced anxiety—not rigid adherence to any particular system.

These tools succeed because they honor how your child's brain works, creating an environment where communication flows naturally rather than feeling like constant translation. When you meet your child in their visual language, you're building connection through understanding—and that's where real progress lives.

9

RELEASING GUILT AND BUILDING SUSTAINABLE PARENT CONFIDENCE

UNDERSTANDING THE ROOTS OF PARENTAL GUILT

Cultural and Societal Pressures

When your child had that meltdown at the grocery store last week, did you notice the looks? The sideways glances from the woman in line behind you, the subtle head shake from the cashier, the way that other parent quickly steered their cart to a different aisle. Those moments aren't just uncomfortable—they're where parental guilt takes root and spreads.

What nobody tells you is that the guilt you're carrying probably has less to do with your actual parenting and more to do with invisible scripts you didn't even know you were following.

Society hands parents of autistic children an impossible task: raise a child who doesn't fit the template using instructions written exclusively for the template. The cultural narrative around "good parenting" assumes a neurotypical child who responds predictably to standard approaches. When your child doesn't hit the same milestones at the same pace, doesn't self-soothe the expected way, or needs accommodations that look like "special treatment" to outsiders, that narrative turns accusatory. It whispers that you're doing something wrong, that you're too soft or too rigid, too involved or too distant. The standards themselves become a trap because they were never designed with your child in mind, yet you're somehow expected to meet them anyway.

I've watched parents apologize for their child's existence in a hundred small ways. *Sorry he's so loud. Sorry we need to leave early. Sorry she can't sit still like the other kids.* Each apology is a little genuflection to norms that don't serve anyone well.

The expectations extend beyond the child to you. There's an assumption that the "right" parent, with enough dedication and the correct interventions, can make autism less visible. This mythology suggests that differences are problems to be solved rather than variations to be supported. When your child still stims in public, still struggles with transitions, still needs the specific blue cup—not the red one, never the red one—it registers as your failure.

The measuring stick itself is broken, but you're the one who feels broken.

Cultural pressure doesn't arrive with a formal announcement. It seeps in through playground conversations, through well-meaning relatives who ask when your child will "catch up," through social media highlight reels of neurotypical milestones. This isolation is real and documented: in a landmark Columbia University study, 32% of parents reported being actively excluded from social activities, while 95% felt the weight of public stigma (Kinnear et al., 2016). It accumulates in the parenting books that don't mention your reality, the birthday parties you stop getting invited to, the preschool teacher who sighs just a little too heavily during pickup.

These external narratives don't just create guilt—they create a fog that obscures what's actually happening in your relationship with your child.

Internalized Myths and Misconceptions

One of the most persistent myths is that good parenting should make autism less apparent. This belief operates on the assumption that visible autistic traits—stimming, sensory sensitivities, communication differences—reflect inadequate intervention or insufficient parental effort. The myth equates your child's neurological reality with your competence as a parent. When your eight-year-old still flaps their hands when excited or your teenager still needs noise-canceling headphones at the mall, this framework interprets those needs as evidence you haven't done enough.

That's not how neurodevelopment works.

Strengths-based support starts from a fundamentally different premise: growth happens through building on your child's strengths and natural development, not by eliminating traits that make them autistic. This approach recognizes that supporting a child means creating environments where they can develop their full potential while remaining authentically themselves.

A 2025 study in the journal *Autism* highlights that prioritizing these strengths fosters higher self-esteem and social connection (White et al., 2025) (White et al., 2025). It's not about making autism invisible—it's about helping your child navigate the world with tools that actually fit their neurology.

Another myth whispers that if you were truly attuned to your child, you'd prevent every meltdown, anticipate every trigger, create perfect conditions at all times. This impossibility standard sets you up for constant failure because meltdowns aren't always preventable. Sometimes your child has reached their sensory limit.

Sometimes the routine changed unexpectedly. Sometimes their nervous system just needs to reset, and no amount of perfect parenting prevents that physiological reality.

Then there's the belief that accepting your child as they are means giving up on progress. I hear this one constantly, usually phrased as concern: *But if I'm not pushing them, how will they grow?* The false dichotomy suggests you must choose between acceptance and development, as if honoring your child's neurology means abandoning all goals.

Acceptance and growth aren't opposites—they're partners. When you accept your child's autistic neurology as a starting point rather than an obstacle, you can identify supports that actually help instead of interventions designed to create a neurotypical facade.

You're not lowering expectations; you're redirecting energy toward meaningful development that respects who your child actually is. That might mean celebrating your child learning to communicate their needs through AAC instead of pushing for spoken words that may never come easily. It might mean teaching self-advocacy skills instead of forced eye contact, which neurological research from Massachusetts General Hospital shows can trigger extreme over-arousal and brain-level distress (Hadjikhani et al., 2017).

These myths don't just create guilt—they actively interfere with the connection your child needs most.

Personal Experiences and Comparisons

Social media serves up a particularly poisonous brand of comparison. Research shows that exposure to curated parenting content is linked to increased role overload, lower feelings of competence, and higher rates of maternal depression (Coyne et al., 2017). The comparison itself becomes the problem—not your actual parenting, but the mental habit of measuring your reality against someone else's highlight reel.

Your guilt also feeds on your own upbringing. If your childhood home valued narrow definitions of achievement—academic ribbons, social popularity, athletic trophies—watching your child follow a completely different developmental path can trigger subconscious disappointment. Not because you love your child any less, but because your internal measuring stick was calibrated to metrics that simply don't apply here. That misalignment isn't your child's failure. It isn't yours, either.

It's just outdated programming.

When you catch yourself thinking, "Other families seem to have it easier," pause and ask: *Easier according to whom?* What if the family you're comparing yourself to is struggling just as deeply, but in ways you can't see? What if their child's progress looks linear only because you're viewing it from the outside, where setbacks and meltdowns and late-night worry sessions remain invisible?

Comparison steals the oxygen from acceptance. It keeps you locked in a cycle of perceived inadequacy, forever chasing a version of parenting that doesn't exist. Your family's journey is not less meaningful because it looks different. It's simply yours—complex, imperfect, and worthy of honoring exactly as it unfolds.

Releasing comparison doesn't mean ignoring helpful advice or closing yourself off from community support. It means choosing self-compassion over judgment, and recognizing that your child's unique path requires your presence, not your perfection.

~

MINDSET SHIFTS FOR RELEASING SELF-DOUBT AND FEAR

Understanding Your Inner Critic

Every parent carries an internal voice that shapes how they see themselves. Sometimes this voice offers guidance and wisdom. But more often, especially when navigating the complexities of parenting an autistic child, it becomes harsh and unforgiving—a relentless critic questioning every decision, every moment of frustration, and every interaction that didn't go as planned; indeed, research shows that parents of autistic children often report lower levels of self-compassion and heightened parenting stress compared to parents of neurotypical children (Liang et al., 2025).

This inner critic doesn't announce itself as an enemy. It disguises itself as protectiveness, whispering that if you just criticize yourself enough, you'll somehow become the perfect parent your child deserves. It tells you that other parents have it figured out, that you're falling behind, that your child's struggles reflect your inadequacy. These thoughts feel like truth, but they're actually fear wearing the mask of protection.

The first step in silencing this voice is recognizing it for what it is: a pattern of negative self-talk rooted in unrealistic expectations and cultural narratives that don't serve your family. Notice when these thoughts arise. Do they sound like your own authentic voice, or do they echo external judgments? Are they helping you connect with your child, or are they creating distance through shame and anxiety?

Once you've identified these critical thoughts, you can begin the work of replacing them with compassionate narratives that align with your family's reality. Instead of "I should have known better," try "I'm learning alongside my child, and that's enough." Rather than "I'm failing them," practice "I'm showing up every day with love and intention." These aren't empty affirmations—they're truthful reframings that honor your effort and your child's unique journey. (Neff & Faso, 2015)

Building this new internal dialogue takes time and deliberate practice. Write down the critical thoughts when they surface, then consciously craft a gentler response. Share these struggles with trusted friends or support groups who understand. Over time, this compassionate voice becomes stronger, creating space for the connection and empathy that truly support your child's growth.

Reframing Parenting Challenges

When Clara's five-year-old son began refusing to leave the house each morning, her immediate thought was *I've done something wrong.* She ran through everything: Was it her tone? Her inconsistency with the visual schedule? Had she pushed too hard last week when he'd actually made it to preschool three days in a row? This spiral consumed her evenings, leaving little room to actually observe what her son needed.

Then her therapist asked a different question: "What if this isn't about your failure? What if he's telling you something important about his capacity right now?"

That single reframe shifted everything. Clara stopped cataloging her mistakes and started noticing patterns. Her son's refusals coincided with construction noise near the school entrance. His nervous system wasn't rejecting her parenting—it was protecting him from sensory overload she hadn't yet identified. Once she requested a quieter drop-off location, his resistance diminished within days. The problem had never been her competence; it was her assumption that challenges automatically indicated parental failure.

Research on parental self-efficacy supports this shift. When parents believe in their capacity to understand and manage caregiving challenges, they report lower stress levels and greater competence (Jones & Prinz, 2005). This isn't about positive thinking masking real struggles—it's about approaching difficulties with curiosity instead of shame. Each behavioral change, each new sensitivity, each unexpected meltdown becomes a data point rather than evidence of inadequacy.

Clara began keeping a simple log: what happened, what might have triggered it, what seemed to help. No judgment, just observation.

Within weeks, patterns emerged she'd never noticed while drowning in self-criticism. Her son wasn't "difficult"—he was communicating through the only channels available to him. This investigative stance doesn't eliminate hard days. But it transforms them from personal failures into collaborative puzzles. When you stop asking "What did I do wrong?" and start asking "What is my child experiencing?" the entire emotional landscape shifts.

Growth happens in that space between certainty and blame.

Cultivating Self-Compassion

Self-compassion isn't about letting yourself off the hook—it's about recognizing that you're human, doing difficult work, and deserving of the same kindness you extend to your child.

When you catch yourself spiraling into self-criticism after a rough morning or a meltdown that felt impossible to manage, pause. Notice the tone of your inner voice. Would you speak that way to a friend navigating the same challenges? Most parents wouldn't dream of it. Yet we reserve our harshest judgments for ourselves, convinced that being hard on ourselves somehow makes us better parents. It doesn't. It just makes us exhausted.

Start by naming what you're feeling without judgment. Simply acknowledging "I'm feeling overwhelmed" or "I'm doubting myself right now" creates space between you and the emotion. It's not about dismissing your feelings or pretending everything is fine—it's about observing them with curiosity rather than condemnation.

One practical exercise is the self-compassion break, a technique adapted from researcher Kristin Neff's work (Neff, 2011). When you notice self-doubt creeping in, place one hand over your heart and take three deep breaths. Then say to yourself: *"This is hard. Other parents feel this way too. May I be kind to myself in this moment."* It might feel awkward at first, but repetition builds genuine self-kindness.

Another powerful shift is reframing your internal narrative. Instead of "I should have handled that better," try "I did my best with what I knew in that moment, and I'm learning." This isn't about lowering standards—it's about replacing the shame that keeps you stuck with the grace that allows you to grow.

Self-compassion also means giving yourself permission to rest, to ask for help, and to acknowledge that you can't pour from an empty cup. When you nurture yourself, you model resilience and self-respect for your child. You show them that everyone—including parents—deserves compassion, patience, and the space to be imperfect.

BUILDING CONFIDENCE THROUGH DAILY PRACTICES

Small Wins, Big Impact

Tracking small victories interrupts a well-documented cognitive pattern known as negativity bias (Baumeister et al., 2001; Rozin & Royzman, 2001). Under this evolutionary tendency, negative experiences register with far greater emotional weight than positive ones. Parents naturally remember the hard moments—the public meltdown, the call from school, the chaotic morning—because our brains prioritize stressful events to ensure survival. The small, successful connections simply don't stick unless you deliberately preserve them.

When you write down that your child smiled during breakfast, or that bedtime went smoothly for the first time in a week, you're not just keeping a record. You're creating tangible evidence that progress is happening. Over time, these entries accumulate into a body of proof that counteracts the brain's natural tendency to fixate on what went wrong. On difficult days, when doubt creeps in and you question whether anything you're doing is working, you can return to these pages and see the truth: you *are* making a difference.

Start simple. At the end of each day, jot down one or two moments where connection felt real, even if they lasted only seconds. Maybe your child made eye contact during a conversation. Maybe they tolerated a new texture at lunch without distress. Maybe they asked for help instead of shutting down. These aren't minor details—they're developmental milestones that deserve recognition.

Some parents find it helpful to include why the moment mattered. "Today, she let me sit next to her during her favorite show. That's progress because last month she needed complete space." This reflection deepens your understanding of your child's journey and reinforces your role in supporting it. You're not a passive observer hoping for change; you're an active participant building trust one small interaction at a time.

The practice doesn't require perfection. You don't need a fancy journal or hours of reflection. A simple notebook, a notes app on your phone, or even sticky notes on the fridge work just as well. What matters is consistency—the daily habit of pausing to notice what went right.

Over weeks and months, patterns emerge. You'll begin to see which strategies work best, which times of day feel easiest, and how far you've both come. That growing collection of small wins becomes your strongest defense against guilt and self-doubt, a reminder that sustainable progress is built one quiet victory at a time.

Mindful Morning Rituals

Crafting a morning ritual that grounds you before the day begins doesn't require elaborate preparation or extra time you don't have. It requires intention—a deliberate decision to meet yourself with care before you meet the demands of parenting.

Even five minutes can shift your internal state from reactive to centered.

Start by identifying what you need most. Some parents crave stillness after chaotic nights. Others need movement to shake off residual stress. There's no single right approach, only what genuinely serves you. The key is choosing practices that feel restorative rather than obligatory, something that fills rather than depletes.

Consider this simple framework for building a sustainable morning ritual:

- Breathwork or brief meditation: Three minutes of focused breathing calms the nervous system. Apps like Insight Timer offer guided sessions designed specifically for parents.
- Journaling: Writing three sentences about what you're feeling or hoping for creates emotional clarity. No elaborate reflections needed—just honest acknowledgment.

- Affirmations: Speaking one truthful statement aloud—"I am learning," "I am enough," "I can handle what comes"—interrupts automatic negative thoughts.
- Physical grounding: Stretching, a short walk, or even standing outside for two minutes connects you to your body and breaks the mental loop of worry.
- Gratitude noticing: Mentally noting one specific thing you appreciate—warm coffee, quiet before the household wakes—trains attention toward what's working.

The ritual works best when it happens *before* you check your phone, read emails, or begin the morning routine with your child. Those first moments belong to you. Protecting them isn't selfish; it's strategic. You can't pour from an empty reservoir, and mornings set the emotional tone for everything that follows.

Research published in the *Journal of Child and Family Studies* shows that parents who practice mindfulness report feeling more satisfied in their parenting role and experience fewer power struggles. Carving out even a small morning buffer—just ten minutes of quiet before waking the household—transforms a parent's capacity to respond with calm rather than react with stress.

Your ritual doesn't need to look like anyone else's. It just needs to feel true. And on mornings when it doesn't happen—because sleep was interrupted, or the day started in crisis—you practice the same self-compassion you're building throughout this entire journey.

Tomorrow offers another chance to begin again.

Reflective Evening Practices

Even with the best intentions, reflective practices can stumble. Knowing where parents typically go off track—and how to correct course quickly—makes the difference between abandoning the practice and building something sustainable.

The perfectionism trap is the most common pitfall. You miss two evenings of reflection and decide the whole effort has failed. This all-

or-nothing thinking mirrors the harsh self-judgment this entire chapter works to dismantle. Recovery is simple: start again tonight. No self-flagellation required. Reflective practices aren't about maintaining streaks; they're about creating touchpoints with yourself whenever possible.

Some parents fall into what I call performance journaling—writing what sounds good rather than what's true. Your gratitude list becomes generic ("I'm grateful for my family") instead of specific and felt ("I'm grateful Noah let me hold his hand for ten seconds today without pulling away"). According to research compiled by the *Greater Good Science Center* (2011), focusing on specific, detailed events or people yields significantly greater psychological benefits than writing a broad, superficial list. The practice only works when it is real and deeply personal.

Another common stumble is using reflection as another opportunity for criticism. You review the day and compile evidence of failure: the meltdown you didn't prevent, the accommodation you forgot, the moment you lost patience. This isn't reflection—it's rumination dressed up as self-improvement. If you notice this pattern, physically interrupt it. Close the journal. Take three breaths. Then write one sentence about what you learned, not what you regret. Learning and self-punishment cannot occupy the same space.

Overcomplicating the practice leads many parents to quit before they've really started.

Elaborate systems with multiple prompts, color-coded entries, and structured formats create friction. When reflection feels like homework, it becomes another task on an already overwhelming list. Strip it back. One question works: "What did I notice today?" Write two sentences. That's enough. You can always expand later, but simplicity keeps the door open when you're exhausted.

Sometimes parents avoid reflection altogether because they fear what they'll find—that the day was harder than they want to admit, that they're struggling more than they think they should be. This avoidance is understandable but counterproductive. *Acknowledging difficulty doesn't make it worse; it makes it visible, which makes it manage-*

able. When resistance surfaces, acknowledge it directly: "I don't want to do this tonight because I'm afraid of what I'll feel." Then write anyway, even just one line.

Recovery from any of these pitfalls follows the same principle you're teaching your child: progress isn't linear, and stumbling doesn't erase what you've built. Tomorrow night, you begin again. That's not failure. That's how sustainable practices actually develop.

Community and Connection

Finding your people takes intention. Local support groups, online communities focused on neurodiversity-affirming approaches, even informal text threads with parents who just *get it*—these connections can transform the emotional landscape of your parenting journey. When you share a hard moment with someone who's lived through something similar, you're not just venting. You're building a network of validation, practical wisdom, and mutual encouragement that reminds you you're not alone in this.

The right community doesn't judge your struggles or push compliance-based solutions that don't align with your values. Instead, they celebrate the small wins, offer creative troubleshooting for tough moments, and remind you that progress isn't linear. They understand the exhaustion of reading every subtle cue, the relief of a smooth transition, the heartbreak of a particularly difficult day. This shared understanding creates a foundation of trust that fuels your confidence far more effectively than any parenting manual ever could.

Start small. You don't need a massive support network overnight. One trusted parent friend, one responsive online forum, one monthly meetup where you feel seen and understood—that's enough to begin shifting from isolation to connection. As you engage with others, you'll notice patterns: strategies that worked for their family, reframes that eased their guilt, routines that brought unexpected calm. These insights become part of your toolkit, not as rigid prescriptions but as inspiration for what might work in your unique household.

Community also offers something deeply powerful: perspective. When you're in the thick of a challenging phase, it's easy to lose sight of how far you've come. Hearing other parents reflect on their own journeys—how a child who once struggled with transitions now navigates them with growing ease, how a family found their rhythm after months of trial and error—reminds you that growth unfolds gradually, and that your efforts are building something real and lasting.

10

PROGRESS OVER PERFECTION: SUSTAINING HOPE FOR THE LONG JOURNEY AHEAD

EMBRACING IMPERFECTION AS A PATHWAY TO GROWTH

Letting Go of Perfection

A mother once told me she'd spent three years meticulously tracking every interaction with her autistic daughter—spreadsheets color-coded by successful transitions, failed mealtimes, and "good" versus "bad" social attempts. She believed if she could just identify the perfect combination of supports, routines, and interventions, her daughter would finally be okay. When I asked what changed, she laughed quietly and said, "I realized I was measuring her life like a science experiment, and I'd forgotten to actually live in it with her."

Perfectionism in autism parenting isn't just exhausting—it actively works against the very progress we're chasing. Research by Özbay et al. (2025) demonstrates that parental perfectionism is a strong driver of overcontrolling parenting attitudes in families with autistic children, reinforcing a cycle of rigidity rather than adaptive support. The pursuit of flawless execution creates a persistent undercurrent of failure, where every imperfect morning routine becomes evidence of inadequacy, every public meltdown feels like proof you've missed something critical, every sensory moment at breakfast leaves you second-guessing whether you responded correctly, whether you should have structured the afternoon differently, whether another parent would have handled it better.

But here's what that mindset misses: your child isn't experiencing your parenting as a graded performance.

They're experiencing *you*—the actual human showing up in their life. When you're constantly evaluating yourself against an impossible standard, you're not fully present. You're mentally reviewing what just happened or rehearsing what comes next, monitoring your tone, questioning your choices. That divided attention is precisely what disconnects you from the intuitive responses that actually build trust and connection.

Releasing perfectionism doesn't mean lowering standards or abandoning structure. It means recognizing that growth happens in the messiness, not despite it. The mornings that don't go as planned teach flexibility. The moments when you lose your patience and then repair the relationship afterward model accountability and resilience. Your child learns far more from watching you navigate imperfection with compassion than from witnessing you execute a flawless routine.

Mistakes as Learning Opportunities

Reframing mistakes as growth opportunities fundamentally changes what you pay attention to as a parent. Instead of asking "What did I do wrong?" after a difficult moment, you begin asking "What did we both just learn?" That shift—from judgment to curiosity—creates space for something far more valuable than error-free execution.

Consider what happens when your child struggles with a transition you thought you'd prepared perfectly for. The perfectionist lens sees failure: you missed a sensory trigger, misjudged the timing, didn't provide enough warning. But through a growth lens, that same moment becomes information. Maybe your child needs movement breaks before transitions, not just verbal cues. Maybe the visual schedule works better when they help create it. The mistake isn't evidence of your inadequacy—it's data about what your specific child needs.

Adaptive parenting requires constant recalibration.

What worked last month may not work today. Your child's sensory needs shift as they grow. Their communication abilities expand in unexpected directions. Social situations that once felt manageable suddenly don't. If you're treating each misstep as a personal failing, you're carrying an ever-growing weight of supposed inadequacy. But if you're treating each misstep as feedback, you're building a flexible repertoire of responses that actually matches your child's evolving reality.

The same principle extends to how your child experiences their own learning process. When they see you respond to your own mistakes with self-compassion rather than harsh self-criticism, they internalize a crucial message: growth is supposed to be imperfect. They learn that trying something new and getting it wrong isn't shameful—it's how humans figure things out. This is especially vital for autistic children, who often face relentless pressure to perform neurotypical behaviors correctly the first time. Indeed, research on "social camouflaging" or masking in the Journal of Autism and Developmental Disorders highlights how suppressing natural behaviors to fit neurotypical standards often leads to perfectionistic pressure, anxiety, and profound exhaustion (Hull et al., 2017). Research on social camouflaging in the *Journal of Autism and Developmental Disorders* highlights how suppressing natural behaviors to fit neurotypical standards often leads to perfectionistic pressure, anxiety, and profound exhaustion (Hull et al., 2017).

One father described how he used to hide his parenting uncertainties from his son, believing he needed to project unwavering confidence. Then one evening, after a particularly chaotic sensory meltdown at a restaurant, he sat down with his son and said, "I really didn't handle that well. I should have noticed you were getting overwhelmed sooner. I'm still learning too." His son looked at him with visible relief and said, "So we're both figuring this out?"

Exactly that.

Cultivating a Growth Mindset

When burnout research tells us that mothers of autistic children experience chronic physiological stress comparable to combat soldiers, we're not talking about abstract statistics (Seltzer et al., 2010). We're talking about the cumulative weight of believing every difficult moment reflects personal failure.

Research in the *Journal of Autism and Developmental Disorders* highlights the heavy toll of parenting perfectionism, showing how this relentless pursuit of mistake-free caregiving directly compounds parental burnout (Yan et al., 2025) (Yan et al., 2025). Growth mindset parenting isn't a feel-good addition to your approach—it's a protective factor against the exhaustion that makes you want to quit entirely.

Without it, you're constantly measuring yourself against an impossible standard: the parent who never loses patience, always anticipates sensory overload, perfectly balances therapeutic intervention with childhood joy. That parent doesn't exist. But the belief that they should drives countless parents into shame spirals that accomplish nothing except making tomorrow harder than today. Your child notices this, even when you think you're hiding it well. They absorb your relationship with mistakes, your tolerance for uncertainty, your capacity to try again after things fall apart.

A growth mindset reframes your entire parenting lens. Instead of "I failed because I didn't handle that meltdown perfectly," you shift to "That was hard, and I learned something that might help next time." Instead of "My child should be further along by now," you embrace "We're building skills at our own pace, and every small step counts."

This isn't just semantic difference—it's a fundamental shift in how you metabolize the inevitable challenges. When you model this approach, your child learns that struggling doesn't mean failing. They begin to see setbacks as information rather than indictment. They develop the resilience to keep trying, because effort itself becomes worthy of celebration.

Start small. Notice one moment today where you didn't meet your own expectations, and practice extending yourself the same grace you'd offer a friend. Tomorrow, try again.

~

CREATING A SUSTAINABLE VISION FOR THE FUTURE

Envisioning a Hopeful Future

Visioning with possibility, not prediction. Most parents of autistic children become inadvertent experts at crisis management—the immediate sensory meltdown, the upcoming IEP meeting, next week's family gathering. This reactive stance makes perfect sense when you're genuinely overwhelmed. But living exclusively in problem-solving mode gradually narrows what you believe is possible for your child's future.

Sustainable visioning isn't about predicting outcomes or setting achievement benchmarks. It's about cultivating a mental space where your child's potential exists independent of current limitations. One mother described her shift this way: "I stopped asking 'Will he ever have friends?' and started noticing he lights up around two specific kids at therapy. That observation opened something—maybe friendship looks different than I imagined, and maybe that's not less valuable."

This reframing matters because parental expectations profoundly shape the opportunities children receive. Research on transition-age autistic youth shows that strong parental expectations are powerful, independent predictors of post-school success, significantly mediating outcomes like employment, independent living, and social participation (Kirby, 2016) (Kirby, 2016). When parents hold a high vision of their child's potential, they offer more opportunities, interpret behaviors more generously, and persist longer through setbacks.

Consider the difference between "My child struggles with communication" and "My child is developing their own communication style."

The first statement closes doors; the second opens inquiry. What does their communication look like now? What environments help it flourish? What supports might expand it? When parents shift from deficit-focused assessment to strength-based curiosity, they begin noticing capabilities that were always present but previously invisible.

Co-creating the vision matters as much as having one. As children develop self-awareness, including them in future conversations—however modified for their developmental level—builds agency. A father started asking his seven-year-old autistic daughter simple questions: "What makes you feel proud? What do you wish grown-ups understood about you?" Her answers surprised him. She didn't care about the social skills goals dominating her therapy schedule. She wanted to learn everything about marine biology and have a dog someday.

Those desires became anchor points for a shared vision that honored her actual interests, not his anxieties about her fitting in. Sustainable hope isn't built on wishing your child were different. It's built on genuinely seeing who they're becoming and helping them move toward their own version of a meaningful life.

Setting Realistic Goals

When Maya's parents brought her to occupational therapy, they arrived with a seventeen-page document outlining their vision for her future: independent living by twenty-two, a college degree, meaningful employment, close friendships. Their therapist gently asked what Maya, then eight, actually enjoyed doing. There was a long silence. They genuinely didn't know—they'd been so focused on the destination that they'd stopped noticing the child actually making the journey.

Breaking vision into actionable steps requires starting where your child actually is, not where developmental charts suggest they should be. This family's turning point came when they identified one concrete, present-moment goal: spend fifteen minutes daily doing something Maya chose, without therapeutic agenda. Within weeks, they discovered she loved sorting objects by texture and could focus intensely when given autonomy. That single observation opened pathways they hadn't imagined—occupational goals around fine motor skills suddenly had intrinsic motivation attached.

The ascent-based approach transforms overwhelming aspirations into manageable experiments. Instead of "improve social skills," the goal becomes "facilitate one positive interaction weekly with a preferred peer." Instead of "reduce anxiety," it becomes "identify two environments where she visibly relaxes." These aren't diminished ambitions—they're the actual building blocks of sustainable change.

One father described his shift this way: "I stopped thinking about high school graduation and started thinking about this Thursday." That sounds like lowered expectations, but it's actually strategic decomposition. When he focused on making Thursday's transition to the bus smoother—laying out clothes the night before, playing her preferred music during breakfast—he was practicing the exact skills that compound over years into genuine independence.

Research on goal-setting in pediatric rehabilitation shows that proximal goals—immediate, specific, and attainable targets—produce significantly better outcomes and higher motivation than distal aspirations alone (Pritchard-Wiart et al., 2019). Proximal goals provide frequent feedback, opportunities for course correction, and the reinforcement of visible progress. They prevent the paralysis that comes from staring at a mountain you don't know how to climb.

This approach honors the book's connection-first framework because it roots goals in your child's actual responses rather than external benchmarks. You're not asking "Is she developing typically?" but "What did I notice brought her joy this week? What small challenge did she navigate? What support helped?" Those observations become your roadmap.

A child who successfully requested a break using their communication device once doesn't need a goal about requesting breaks fifty times. They need you to notice what made that one success possible —and gently expand those conditions.

Nurturing Resilience Through Challenges

Resilience in autism parenting isn't about enduring hardship with a brave face. It's about developing specific practices that protect your capacity to show up, even when progress feels invisible.

One mother described keeping a "proof jar"—each time her son demonstrated a skill that felt impossible months earlier, she dropped a small stone into a glass container on her kitchen counter. During particularly difficult weeks, she'd hold that jar and physically feel the weight of accumulated growth. Build a resilience anchor: one concrete practice that reconnects you to progress when you're drowning in setbacks. This might be a voice memo you record after small victories, a photo album on your phone documenting successful moments, or a simple notebook where you write one thing that worked today. The format matters less than creating a tangible record your brain can access when emotional exhaustion makes everything feel futile. Research on caregiver resilience confirms that parents who cultivate positive cognitions—or specific positive thinking patterns—experience significantly greater psychological resourcefulness and coping capacity (Bekhet et al., 2012).

This resourcefulness isn't an innate personality trait you either possess or lack—it's a skill you practice. When your child has been awake screaming for three hours and you've tried every sensory strategy you know, resilience isn't pretending everything's fine. It's remembering that two months ago these episodes lasted five hours, and you didn't know about weighted blankets yet. That comparison isn't minimizing current pain—it's building accurate perspective against the brain's negativity bias.

Without deliberate practices, our minds naturally emphasize what's wrong and dismiss incremental improvements as insignificant. A child who now tolerates the grocery store for twelve minutes instead of eight isn't "still struggling with shopping"—they've expanded their window by fifty percent.

Resilience also means knowing when to stop trying and just survive the moment.

Not every meltdown needs analysis. Not every difficult day requires extracting a lesson. Sometimes the most sustainable response is: "That was terrible, we got through it, and tomorrow's a different day." Releasing the pressure to optimize every experience is itself a form of endurance. One father keeps a document titled "Things I Thought Would Never Change But Did." Reading it doesn't erase current struggles—but it reminds him that his predictions about permanence have been wrong before.

BUILDING A SUPPORT NETWORK FOR CONTINUOUS HOPE

Identifying Key Support Figures

Start by listing three people who already know your child well enough to notice their growth, not just their challenges. This might be a grandparent who celebrates your daughter's encyclopedic knowledge of trains, a neighbor who waves specifically at your son each morning, or a therapist who texts you unprompted when they see progress you've missed.

Write their names down. Then add one concrete way each person already supports you—not theoretically, but actually. "Brings dinner without asking if we need it" counts more than *"would probably help if I asked."*

Now identify one person you wish understood better. Not someone to convert or convince, but someone whose support would genuinely lighten your load if they grasped what your daily reality looks like. Maybe it's your partner, who sees the meltdowns but not the sensory overload that preceded them. Maybe it's a family member who loves your child deeply but defaults to compliance-based advice that doesn't fit your framework.

Consider what small shift in their understanding might create meaningful change. You're not asking them to become an autism expert overnight. You're identifying one specific way they could show up differently—like pausing before offering advice, or noticing when your child self-regulates instead of only commenting when things go sideways.

The strongest support networks aren't built on people who have all the answers. They're built on people who affirm your child's worth, respect your intuition as a parent, and show up consistently in ways that actually help. When you surround yourself with individuals who understand neurodiversity as difference rather than deficit, you create a foundation that sustains hope not just for this week or this month, but for the entire journey ahead.

Creating Mutual Support Systems

Building reciprocal support doesn't mean maintaining perfectly balanced scorecards of who helped whom last. It means recognizing that the parent who understands why your child won't eat anything green this month might desperately need someone who gets why their son's new scripting pattern feels overwhelming.

One mother described her turning point: a friend whose daughter was also autistic asked if she could vent about a disastrous school meeting. For the first time in months, this mother wasn't the one explaining, justifying, or requesting understanding. She was the person who already knew. When she offered a specific strategy that had worked in her own IEP negotiations, her friend's relief was palpable—but so was her own. Being needed restored something that constant advocacy had eroded. She wasn't just the parent who required accommodation and patience. She had developed hard-won expertise worth sharing.

Reciprocal networks thrive when parents recognize they're simultaneously learning and teaching. You might know nothing about communication devices but everything about navigating insurance denials. Another parent has mastered visual schedules but desperately needs insight into sibling dynamics you've spent three years figuring out. This exchange matters beyond practical problem-solving. A systematic review of peer support by Shilling et al.

(2013) highlighted that giving support is just as vital as receiving it, fostering a profound sense of reciprocity and mutuality (Shilling et al., 2013). When you're always receiving help, you can start feeling like a project. When you're only giving it, you burn out. Reciprocity preserves dignity on both sides.

Start noticing what you've learned that might genuinely help someone else. Not polished advice—*specific things that worked.* The exact weighted blanket brand that survived your child's chewing. How you finally got the school to stop pulling your daughter from music class for social skills instruction. The phrase that helps your mother-in-law pause before offering unhelpful suggestions.

One father who volunteered with a local parent-to-parent network experienced this shift firsthand. After years of feeling like the passive recipient of clinical advice, he began mentoring other families. Sharing his practical strategies for sensory regulation and school advocacy allowed him to see his own hard-won knowledge as valuable. Watching other parents succeed rebuilt a deep confidence that he wasn't just surviving this journey, but actually learning how to navigate it.

Reciprocal support also means letting people contribute in ways that match their actual capacity, not your idealized wish list.

Leveraging Community Resources

These practices—finding community resources, building reciprocal relationships, anchoring yourself in specific support structures—

aren't separate tasks you add to an already impossible schedule. They're protective infrastructure that makes the schedule itself more sustainable. When you know Thursday's therapy carpool is covered, when you've got three parents who understand why this week has been brutal, when you've bookmarked that online forum where someone always responds within an hour, you're not parenting in a vacuum anymore.

Community resources work best when they're treated as living systems you adjust over time, not fixed solutions you implement once. The support group that felt perfect when your child was four might feel irrelevant at nine. The online forum that saved you during the diagnosis period might become overwhelming when you need less crisis support and more long-term planning conversation. As your child's developmental needs evolve, your support network must evolve with them.

What matters most isn't finding the perfect community. It's recognizing that isolation is a choice you can unmake, incrementally, through small experiments that test what actually helps. Posting one question in an online group. Attending one workshop. Saying yes when another parent suggests coffee.

In structured parent-to-parent mentoring models—such as those evaluated in a comprehensive 2024 review in the journal *Autism*—experienced parent mentors often discover an unexpected benefit: *their own sense of progress becomes clearer* when they articulate strategies to someone else (Lee et al., 2024) (Lee et al., 2024). Explaining how they learned to recognize early sensory distress signals or advocate for school accommodations forces mentors to acknowledge how far their own skills have developed. They aren't just helping other families; they are reinforcing evidence of their own resilience.

Progress in autism parenting rarely announces itself with clear milestones.

It accumulates quietly in competencies you don't notice until you're sharing them. In connections that started as desperate resource-gathering and became genuine friendship. In the shift from "I can't do this" to "I've done harder things than this before." Building support networks isn't about achieving some ideal state of connectedness. It's about reducing the friction between struggle and help—making it slightly easier to reach out, slightly more likely someone understands, slightly less exhausting to keep going. And discovering, sometimes to your surprise, that the help you offer might sustain you as much as the help you receive.

AFTERWORD

When you first opened these pages, you might have been sitting in a quiet room, exhausted from another long day of navigating invisible boundaries, wondering if you were doing any of this right. Perhaps your home felt like a minefield of unpredictable sensory storms, and the well-meaning advice of traditional parenting guides only left you feeling more isolated, burdened by a heavy cloak of parental guilt. You wanted answers, yes, but more than that, you wanted a sense of peace and a way to truly reach your child. Now, as we stand at the threshold of this final chapter, that overwhelming fog has begun to lift, replaced by the quiet confidence of a parent who has learned to stop managing behaviors and start nurturing a human soul. You have shifted your gaze from compliance to connection, and in doing so, you have already altered the emotional landscape of your home. You are no longer just reacting to a crisis; you are building a safe harbor.

Looking back at where you started, it is easy to see how the relentless pressure to enforce conformity can drain the joy out of family life. You used to find yourself caught in the exhausting cycle of trying to fit a beautifully unique, neurodivergent child into a rigid, compliance-first mold that was never designed for them. Today, you hold a completely different map of your child's inner world, one that respects their sensory processing differences, values their developmental timeline, and treats emotional dysregulation not as a behavioral rebellion, but as a direct distress signal from an overloaded nervous system. This change in perspective is nothing short of revolutionary, representing a profound act of love that honors who your child actually is rather than who society expects them to be. You now understand that when a child feels safe, their behavior naturally aligns with their development, eliminating the need for force.

By laying down the heavy burden of trying to "fix" your child, you have opened up space for genuine connection to flourish, creating a home environment where both of you can finally breathe. Throughout this book, we have explored how real, lasting progress is built upon the solid bedrock of the Ascent Framework, a philosophy that prioritizes trust, emotional safety, and relational attunement over simple behavioral control. We began by deconstructing the harmful limitations of compliance-based metrics, realizing that a child's outward obedience should never come at the expense of their internal security. By understanding that your child's brain interprets sensory inputs in highly specific, sometimes intense ways, you have unlocked the ability to read the subtle body language and non-verbal cues that precede emotional overload.

We looked closely at the delicate architecture of the nervous system, learning to decode the early signs of dysregulation so that we can intervene with soothing support long before a meltdown ever begins. This proactive stance changes everything, shifting your role from a behavioral warden to an empathetic guide who anticipates needs rather than punishes outcomes. Equipped with this knowledge, you have seen how predictable daily rituals and scheduled sensory breaks act as emotional anchors, giving your child the environmental stability they need to explore, learn, and grow. We dismantled the traditional response to meltdowns, replacing the urge to control and discipline with a commitment to maintaining your own calm and offering radical, de-escalating compassion.

By utilizing visual aids, personalized social stories, and communication strategies that respect your child's natural language, you have built functional bridges where there once were walls of frustration. This holistic approach ensures that every interaction, from the chaotic rush of a Monday morning to the quiet routine of bedtime, is infused with opportunities for shared joy and mutual understanding. You are no longer measuring success by quiet compliance, but by the depth of trust that exists between you. Consider what the coming months will look like as these practices take deep root in your daily life. Picture your living room not as a space of tension and unpredictable outbursts, but as a calm harbor where your child feels safe to express their needs, navigate their sensory spikes, and slowly find their footing.

You will find yourself pausing before you react, using your mindful presence to co-regulate with your child during moments of stress rather than escalating the tension with demands for compliance. When challenges arise—as they inevitably will—you will not see them as parenting failures, but as gentle invitations to deepen your attunement and adapt the environment to support your child's nervous system. Your relationship will transform into a collaborative partnership, where growth happens naturally because the fear of judgment has been entirely removed from the equation. This shift not only relieves the pressure on your child, but also restores your own sense of joy and purpose as a parent.

As your child grows within this trust-based environment, they will begin to internalize the emotional safety you have so carefully constructed for them. They will start to recognize their own sensory limits, using the emotional vocabulary and self-regulation tools you have taught them to advocate for themselves before their nervous system is overwhelmed. Imagine watching them confidently navigate a crowded family gathering or a transition at school, knowing they have a safe parent to return to and a deep-seated belief in their own worth. This is the ultimate gift of the connection-first mindset: you are not just managing their childhood; you are equipping them with the self-awareness, resilience, and confidence they will carry with them for the rest of their lives. They will learn to view their own neurodivergent mind not as a deficit to be corrected, but as a unique strength to be explored, enabling them to navigate the wider world on their own terms.

To turn these concepts into your lived reality, you must transition from passive reading to intentional, daily action, beginning with a single step that you can take before this day ends. I want you to identify one consistent daily transition that currently causes friction in your home—whether it is waking up, leaving the house, or preparing for bed—and design a simple, comforting ritual around it. This could involve creating a clear visual schedule, introducing a comforting sensory tool, or dedicating five minutes of uninterrupted, child-led play before the transition begins. The key is to make this small change predictable and entirely free of pressure, allowing your child to experience a sense of safety and collaboration rather than an abrupt demand. Doing this consistently creates neural pathways of safety that will gradually transform how they handle change, turning moments of dread into opportunities for shared connection.

Your next immediate task is to assemble a personalized sensory toolkit with your child, selecting a few specific items that bring them comfort and help them regulate their nervous system. Gather these tools—perhaps some noise-canceling headphones, a tactile toy, or a weighted lap pad—and place them in an easily accessible, designated "calm corner" of your home. Show your child this space during a moment of calm, explaining without pressure that these tools are always there to help their body feel safe and grounded whenever things feel a bit too loud or overwhelming. By proactively organizing this physical resource today, you are sending a powerful message to your child that their sensory experiences are real, valid, and worthy of proactive care. It is a physical manifestation of your commitment to their comfort, proving to them that you are active partners in their emotional well-being.

Please remember, as you implement these strategies, that you are not aiming for flawless parenting, nor should you expect your child to achieve a state of permanent, unbroken regulation. Progress in the neurodivergent world is rarely a straight, upward line; it is a beautiful, sometimes messy spiral of forward steps, sudden plateaus, and occasional regressions. When a meltdown occurs or when you lose your temper after an exhausting day, this is not a sign that the Ascent Framework has failed, or that you are a bad parent. It is simply a reminder that you are human, and that connection is built on repair, not on the absence of conflict. Every time you apologize, validate your child's feelings, and work to rebuild trust after a difficult moment, you are modeling the exact emotional resilience they need to see. You are teaching them that relationships can bend without breaking, and that love is strong enough to survive the stormiest of days.

You already possess the most important tool required to guide your child through this journey, and that is your own intuitive, deeply felt love for them. No clinical specialist, therapy program, or external expert knows your child's unique heart, fears, and sparks of joy better than you do. Trust that quiet inner voice that tells you when a strategy is not working, and have the courage to discard traditional compliance methods that feel cold or disconnecting to your parenting soul. You have the knowledge, the framework, and the deep empathy needed to build a life of mutual respect and understanding, so let go of the comparison traps and step into your role with absolute confidence. Your child does not need a perfect parent; they simply need a present, attuned advocate who refuses to give up on their connection, standing by them with open arms through every phase of their growth.

At its core, supporting an autistic child is not about fixing a broken system, but about adjusting the frequency of our own hearts so we can find a common language. The Ascent Framework is not a set of rigid rules to enforce, but a gentle pathway of trust that allows your child to rise to their fullest potential at their own pace, securely anchored by your unwavering presence. When we stop demanding that our children conform to a world they do not understand, we open the door for them to show us a world of breathtaking depth, creativity, and unique beauty. It is in these quiet, attuned spaces of mutual understanding that the real magic of parenting happens, where both parent and child are transformed. By shifting your focus from managing behaviors to building a deep, unbreakable bond, you are giving your child the ultimate foundation for a fulfilling life.

As you close this book and step back into the wonderful, lived reality of your home, carry with you the certainty that you are more than enough for your child, just as they are more than enough for you. Your willingness to listen, to learn, and to meet them with compassion instead of control is the most transformative force in their lives. Keep moving forward, one small daily ritual, one gentle breath, and one moment of connection at a time. The road ahead may have its twists and challenges, but you are no longer walking it in the dark; you are guided by the light of trust, and that is a light that will never fail to show you the way home.

BIBLIOGRAPHY

American Psychiatric Association. (2013). Diagnostic and statistical manual of mental disorders (5th ed.). American Psychiatric Association. https://doi.org/10.1176/appi.books.9780890425596

Attfield, I., Fowler, A., & Jones, V. (2016). Sensory Audit for Schools and Classrooms. Autism Education Trust.

Azhari, A., Bizzego, A., & Esposito, G. (2019). Parenting stress undermines mother-child brain-to-brain synchrony: A hyperscanning study. Scientific Reports, 9(1), 11407. https://doi.org/10.1038/s41598-019-47810-4

Bekhet, A. K., Johnson, N. L., & Zauszniewski, J. A. (2012). Effects on resilience of caregivers of persons with autism spectrum disorder: The role of positive cognitions. Journal of the American Psychiatric Nurses Association, 18(6), 337–344. https://doi.org/10.1177/1078390312467056

Bemmouna, D., & Weiner, L. (2023). Linehan's biosocial model applied to emotion dysregulation in autism: a narrative review of the literature and an illustrative case conceptualization. *Frontiers in Psychiatry*, 14, 1238116. https://doi.org/10.3389/fpsyt.2023.1238116

Ben-Sasson, A., Carter, A. S., & Briggs-Gowan, M. J. (2009). Sensory Over-Responsivity in Elementary School: Prevalence and Social-Emotional Correlates. Journal of Abnormal Child Psychology, 37(5), 705–716. https://doi.org/10.1007/s10802-008-9295-8

Bird, G., & Cook, R. (2013). Mixed emotions: the contribution of alexithymia to the emotional symptoms of autism. Translational Psychiatry, 3(7), e285.

Bodison, S. C., & Parham, L. D. (2018). Specific sensory techniques and sensory environmental modifications for children and youth with sensory integration difficulties: A systematic review. The American Journal of Occupational Therapy, 72(1), 7201190040p1-7201190040p11. https://doi.org/10.5014/ajot.2018.029413

Bogdashina, O. (2003). Sensory perceptual issues in autism and Asperger syndrome: Different sensory experiences - different perceptual worlds. Jessica Kingsley Publishers.

Bornstein, M. H., & Esposito, G. (2023). Coregulation: A Multilevel Approach via Biology and Behavior. Children, 10(8), 1323. https://doi.org/10.3390/children10081323

Breaux, C. A., & Smith, K. (2023). Assent in applied behaviour analysis and positive behaviour support: ethical considerations and practical recommendations. International Journal of Developmental Disabilities, 69(1), 111–121. https://doi.org/10.1080/20473869.2022.2144969

Brewer, R., Biotti, F., Catmur, C., Press, C., Happé, F., Cook, R., & Bird, G. (2016). Can neurotypical individuals read autistic facial expressions? Atypical production of emotional facial expressions in Autism Spectrum Disorders. Autism Research, 9(2), 262–271. https://doi.org/10.1002/aur.1508

Cage, E., Di Monaco, J., & Newell, V. (2018). Experiences of autism acceptance and mental health in autistic adults. Journal of Autism and Developmental Disorders, 48(2), 473–484. https://doi.org/10.1007/s10803-017-3342-7

Corbett, B. A., Schupp, C. W., Levine, S., & Mendoza, S. (2009). Comparing cortisol, stress, and sensory sensitivity in children with autism. Autism Research, 2(1), 39–49. https://doi.org/10.1002/aur.64

Crain, W. (2024). Theories of development: Concepts and applications (7th ed.). Routledge. https://doi.org/10.4324/9781003315483

Cymbiotika. (2026). How Long Does Stress Take to Leave Your Body? Understanding the Timeline. Cymbiotika. https://cymbiotika.com

Deel, N. M., Brodhead, M. T., Akers, J. S., White, A. N., & Miranda, D. R. G. (2021). Teaching choice-making within activity schedules to children with autism. Behavioral Interventions, 36(4), 731–744. https://doi.org/10.1002/bin.1816

Delahooke, M. (2019). Beyond behaviors: Using brain science and compassion to understand and solve children's behavioral challenges. PESI Publishing & Media.

Delahooke, M. (2022). Brain-body parenting: How to stop managing behavior and start raising joyful, resilient kids. Harper Wave.

Desautels, L. L. (2020). Connections over compliance: Rewiring our perceptions of discipline. Wyatt-MacKenzie Publishing.

Dettmer, S., Simpson, R. L., Myles, B. S., & Ganz, J. B. (2000). The Use of Visual Supports to Facilitate Transitions of Students with Autism. Focus on Autism and Other Developmental Disabilities, 15(3), 163–169. https://doi.org/10.1177/108835760001500307

Doherty, M., McCowan, S., & Shaw, S. C. (2023). Autistic SPACE: a novel framework for meeting the needs of autistic people in healthcare settings. British Journal of Hospital Medicine, 84(4), 1–9. https://doi.org/10.12968/hmed.2023.0006

Dunn, W. (1997). The Impact of Sensory Processing Abilities on the Daily Lives of Young Children and Their Families: A Conceptual Model. Infants & Young Children, 9(4), 23–35. https://doi.org/10.1097/00001163-199704000-00005

Dunn, W. (1999). Sensory Profile: User's Manual. Psychological Corporation.

Everyday Speech. (2025). How to set neurodiverse-affirming IEP goals. Everyday Speech. https://everydayspeech.com/blog/iep-goals/how-to-set-neurodiverse-affirming-iep-goals/

Fivush, R., Haden, C. A., & Reese, E. (2006). Elaborating on Elaborations: Role of Maternal Reminiscing Style in Cognitive and Socioemotional Development. Child Development, 77(6), 1568–1588. https://doi.org/10.1111/j.1467-8624.2006.00960.x

Gee, D. G., & Cohodes, E. M. (2021). Influences of Caregiving on Development: A Sensitive Period for Biological Embedding of Predictability and Safety Cues. Current Directions in Psychological Science, 30(5), 376-383. https://doi.org/10.1177/09637214211015673

Gerritsen, R. J. S., & Band, G. P. H. (2018). Breath of Life: The Respiratory Vagal Stimulation Model of Contemplative Activity. Frontiers in Human Neuroscience, 12, 397. https://doi.org/10.3389/fnhum.2018.00397

Gessaroli, E., Santelli, E., di Pellegrino, G., & Frassinetti, F. (2013). Personal space regulation in childhood autism spectrum disorders. PLoS ONE, 8(9), e74959. https://doi.org/10.1371/journal.pone.0074959

Gottman, J., & DeClaire, J. (1997). Raising an Emotionally Intelligent Child: The Heart of Parenting. Simon & Schuster.

Gourley, L., Wind, C., Henninger, E. M., & Chinitz, S. (2013). Sensory processing difficulties, behavioral problems, and parental stress in a clinical population of young children. Journal of Child and Family Studies, 22(7), 912–921. https://doi.org/10.1007/s10826-012-9650-9

Gray, C. A., & Garand, J. D. (1993). Social stories: Improving responses of students with autism with accurate social information. Focus on Autistic Behavior, 8(1), 1-10. https://doi.org/10.1177/108835769300800101

Greene, R. W. (2014). Lost at school: Why our kids with behavioral challenges are falling through the cracks and how we can help them (Revised 2nd ed.). Scribner.

Greene, R. W. (2021). The explosive child: A new approach for understanding and parenting easily frustrated, chronically inflexible children (6th ed.). Harper Paperbacks.

Gross, J. J. (1998). The emerging field of emotion regulation: An integrative review. Review of General Psychology, 2(3), 271–299. https://doi.org/10.1037/1089-2680.2.3.271

Hadjikhani, N., Åsberg Johnels, J., Zürcher, N. R., Lassalle, A., Guillon, Q., Hippolyte, L., Billstedt, E., Ward, N., Lemonnier, E., & Gillberg, C. (2017). Look me in the eyes: constraining gaze in the eye-region provokes abnormally high subcortical activation in autism. Scientific Reports, 7(1), 3163. https://doi.org/10.1038/s41598-017-03378-5

Hadjikhani, N., Åsberg Johnels, J., Zürcher, N. R., Lassalle, A., Guillon, Q., Hippolyte, L., Billstedt, E., Ward, N., Lemonnier, E., & Gillberg, C. (2017). Look me in the eyes: constraining gaze in the eye-region provokes abnormally high subcortical activation in autism. Scientific Reports, 7(1), 3163. https://doi.org/10.1038/s41598-017-03378-5

Harlan, B., & Thomad, S. (2022, October 17). The 5-minute daily playtime ritual that can get your kids to listen better. NPR Life Kit. https://www.npr.org/2022/10/13/1128737199/the-5-minute-daily-playtime-ritual-that-can-get-your-kids-to-listen-better

Hull, L., Petrides, K. V., Allison, C., Smith, P., Baron-Cohen, S., Lai, M.-C., & Mandy, W. (2017). "Putting on My Best Normal": Social Camouflaging in Adults with Autism Spectrum Conditions. Journal of Autism and Developmental Disorders, 47(8), 2519–2534. https://doi.org/10.1007/s10803-017-3166-5

Ivey, M. L., Heflin, L. J., & Alberto, P. (2004). The use of social stories to promote independent behaviors in novel events for children with PDD-NOS. Focus on Autism and Other Developmental Disabilities, 19(3), 164-176. https://doi.org/10.1177/10883576040190030401

Jones, T. L., & Prinz, R. J. (2005). Potential roles of parental self-efficacy in parent and child adjustment: a review. Clinical Psychology Review, 25(3), 341–363. https://doi.org/10.1016/j.cpr.2004.12.004

Kabat-Zinn, M., & Kabat-Zinn, J. (1997). *Everyday Blessings: The Inner Work of Mindful Parenting*. Hyperion.

Kapp, S. K., Steward, R., Crane, L., Elliott, D., Elphick, C., Pellicano, E., & Russell, G. (2019). 'People should be allowed to do what they like': Autistic adults' views and experiences of stimming. Autism, 23(7), 1782-1792. https://doi.org/10.1177/1362361319829628

Kennedy, B. (2022). Good Inside: A Practical Guide to Resilient Parenting Prioritizing Connection Over Correction. Harper Wave.

Kilroy, E., Aziz-Zadeh, L., & Cermak, S. (2019). Ayres Theories of Autism and Sensory Integration Revisited: What Contemporary Neuroscience Has to Say. Brain Sciences, 9(3), 68. https://doi.org/10.3390/brainsci9030068

Kinnaird, E., Stewart, C., & Tchanturia, K. (2019). Investigating alexithymia in autism: A systematic review and meta-analysis. European Psychiatry, 55, 80–89. https://doi.org/10.1016/j.eurpsy.2018.09.004

Kinnear, S. H., Link, B. G., Ballan, M. S., & Fischbach, R. L. (2016). Understanding the experience of stigma for parents of children with autism spectrum disorder and the role stigma plays in families' lives. Journal of Autism and Developmental Disorders, 46(3), 942–953. https://doi.org/10.1007/s10803-015-2637-9

Kirby, A. V. (2016). Parent expectations mediate outcomes for young adults with autism spectrum disorder. Journal of Autism and Developmental Disorders, 46(5), 1643–1655. https://doi.org/10.1007/s10803-015-2691-3

Kochanska, G., Kim, S., Boldt, L. J., & Nordling, J. K. (2013). Promoting Toddlers' Positive Social-Emotional Outcomes in Low-Income Families: A Play-Based Experimental Study. Journal of Clinical Child & Adolescent Psychology, 42(5), 700–712. https://doi.org/10.1080/15374416.2013.782815

Kolb, B., & Gibb, R. (2011). Brain plasticity and behaviour in the developing brain. Journal of the Canadian Academy of Child and Adolescent Psychiatry, 20(4), 265–276.

Kuypers, L. M. (2011). *The Zones of Regulation: A Curriculum Designed to Foster Self-Regulation and Emotional Control*. Think Social Publishing, Inc.

Lambie, J. A., Lambie, H. J., & Sadek, S. (2020). “My child will actually say ‘I am upset’... Before all they would do was scream”: Teaching parents emotion validation in a social care setting. *Child: Care, Health and Development*, 46(5), 627–636. https://doi.org/10.1111/cch.12770

Landreth, G. L. (2012). Play Therapy: The Art of the Relationship (3rd ed.). Routledge. https://doi.org/10.4324/9780203835159

Lee, J. D., Terol, A. K., Yoon, C. D., & Meadan, H. (2024). Parent-to-parent support among parents of children with autism: A review of the literature. Autism, 28(2), 263-275. https://doi.org/10.1177/13623613221146444

Leekam, S. R., Nieto, C., Libby, S. J., Wing, L., & Gould, J. (2007). Describing the sensory abnormalities of children and adults with autism. Journal of Autism and Developmental Disorders, 37(5), 894–910. https://doi.org/10.1007/s10803-006-0218-7

Liang, K., Lam, K. K. L., Huang, L., Lin, X., Wang, Z., Liu, H., & Chi, P. (2025). Self-compassion, mental health, and parenting: Comparing parents of autistic and nonautistic children. Autism, 29(1), 53-63.

Lieberman, M. D., Eisenberger, N. I., Crockett, M. J., Tom, S. M., Pfeifer, J. H., & Way, B. M. (2007). Putting feelings into words: affect labeling disrupts amygdala activity in response to affective stimuli. Psychological Science, 18(5), 421–428. https://doi.org/10.1111/j.1467-9280.2007.01916.x

Linehan, M. M. (1993). *Cognitive-Behavioral Treatment of Borderline Personality Disorder*. Guilford Press.

Makris, G., Agorastos, A., Chrousos, G. P., & Pervanidou, P. (2022). Stress system activation in children and adolescents with autism spectrum disorder. Frontiers in Neuroscience, 15, Article 756628. https://doi.org/10.3389/fnins.2021.756628

Marsh, J. (2011, November 17). Tips for Keeping a Gratitude Journal. Greater Good Magazine. Greater Good Science Center at UC Berkeley. https://greatergood.berkeley.edu/article/item/tips_for_keeping_a_gratitude_journal

Meadan, H., Ostrosky, M. M., Triplett, B., Michna, A., & Fettig, A. (2011). Using Visual Supports with Young Children with Autism Spectrum Disorder. TEACHING Exceptional Children, 43(6), 28–35. https://doi.org/10.1177/004005991104300603

Mindell, J. A., & Williamson, A. A. (2018). Benefits of a bedtime routine in young children: Sleep, development, and beyond. Sleep Medicine Reviews, 40, 93–108. https://doi.org/10.1016/j.smrv.2017.10.007

Misevičė, M., Gervinskaitė-Paulaitienė, L., Lesinskienė, S., & Grauslienė, I. (2024). Trust-Based Relational Intervention® (TBRI®) Impact for Traumatized Children—Meaningful Change on Attachment Security and Mental Health after One Year. Children, 11(4), 411. https://doi.org/10.3390/children11040411

Myles, B. S., & Southwick, J. (2005). Asperger Syndrome and Difficult Moments: Practical Solutions for Tantrums, Rage, and Meltdowns (2nd ed.). AAPC Publishing.

National Scientific Council on the Developing Child. (2014). Excessive stress disrupts the architecture of the developing brain: Working paper no. 3 (Updated ed.). Center on the Developing Child at Harvard University. https://developingchild.harvard.edu/resources/wp3/

Neff, K. (2011). Self-compassion: The proven power of being kind to yourself. William Morrow.

Neff, K. D., & Faso, D. J. (2015). Self-compassion and well-being in parents of children with autism. Mindfulness, 6(4), 938-947.

Journal of Child and Family Studies. (2019). Mindful parenting correlates with parenting satisfaction and reduced parent-child conflict.

Nummenmaa, L., Glerean, E., Hari, R., & Hietanen, J. K. (2014). Bodily maps of emotions. Proceedings of the National Academy of Sciences, 111(2), 646-651.

Oberman, L. M., Winkielman, P., & Ramachandran, V. S. (2009). Slow echo: facial EMG evidence for the delay of spontaneous, but not voluntary, emotional mimicry in children with autism spectrum disorders. Developmental Science, 12(4), 510-520. https://doi.org/10.1111/j.1467-7687.2008.00796.x

Parten, M. B. (1932). Social participation among preschool children. Journal of Abnormal and Social Psychology, 27(3), 243–269. https://doi.org/10.1037/h0074524

Perry, B. D., & Szalavitz, M. (2006). *The Boy Who Was Raised as a Dog: And Other

Stories from a Child Psychiatrist's Notebook--What Traumatized Children Can Teach Us About Loss, Love, and Healing*. Basic Books.

Perry, B. D., & Winfrey, O. (2021). What happened to you? Conversations on trauma, resilience, and healing. Flatiron Books.

Pfeiffer, B., Stein Duker, L., Murphy, A., & Shui, C. (2019). Effectiveness of Noise-Attenuating Headphones on Physiological Responses for Children With Autism Spectrum Disorders. Frontiers in Integrative Neuroscience, 13, Article 65. https://doi.org/10.3389/fnint.2019.00065

Porges, S. W. (2004). Neuroception: A subconscious system for detecting threats and safety. Zero to Three, 24(5), 19-24.

Pritchard-Wiart, L., Thompson-Hodgetts, S., & McKillop, A. B. (2019). A review of goal setting theories relevant to goal setting in paediatric rehabilitation. Clinical Rehabilitation, 33(9), 1515–1526. https://doi.org/10.1177/0269215519846220

Prizant, B. M., & Fields-Meyer, T. (2015). Uniquely Human: A Different Way of Seeing Autism. Simon & Schuster.

Prizant, B. M., & Fields-Meyer, T. (2015). Uniquely Human: A Different Way of Seeing Autism. Simon & Schuster.

Reber, D. (2018). Differently wired: Raising an exceptional child in a conventional world. Workman Publishing.

Reese, E., Bird, A., & Tripp, G. (2007). Children's Self-Esteem and Moral Self: Links to Parent-Child Conversations Regarding Emotion. Social Development, 16(3), 460–478. https://doi.org/10.1111/j.1467-9507.2007.00393.x

Reynolds, A. M., & Malow, B. A. (2011). Sleep and autism spectrum disorders. Pediatric Clinics of North America, 58(3), 685–698. https://doi.org/10.1016/j.pcl.2011.03.009

Rutherford, M., Baxter, J., Grayson, Z., Johnston, L., & O'Hare, A. (2020). Visual supports at home and in the community for individuals with autism spectrum disorders: A scoping review. Autism, 24(2), 447–469. https://doi.org/10.1177/1362361319871756

Rutherford, M., Baxter, J., Johnston, L., Tyagi, V., & Maciver, D. (2023). Piloting a home visual support intervention with families of autistic children and children with related needs aged 0–12. International Journal of Environmental Research and Public Health, 20(5), 4401. https://doi.org/10.3390/ijerph20054401

Sandoval-Norton, A. H., & Shkedy, G. (2019). How much compliance is too much compliance: Is long-term ABA therapy abuse? Cogent Psychology, 6(1), Article 1641258. https://doi.org/10.1080/23311908.2019.1641258

Schaaf, R. C., Dumont, R. L., Arbesman, M., & May-Benson, T. A. (2018). Efficacy of Occupational Therapy Using Ayres Sensory Integration®: A Systematic Review. American Journal of Occupational Therapy, 72(1), 7201190010p1-7201190010p10. https://doi.org/10.5014/ajot.2018.028431

Seltzer, M. M., Greenberg, J. S., Hong, J., Smith, L. E., Almeida, D. M., Coe, C., & Stawski, R. S. (2010). Maternal cortisol levels and behavior problems in adolescents and adults with ASD. Journal of Autism and Developmental Disorders, 40(4), 457–469. https://doi.org/10.1007/s10803-009-0887-0

Shah, P., Hall, R., Catmur, C., & Bird, G. (2016). Alexithymia, not autism, is associated with impaired interoception. Cortex, 81, 215–220. https://doi.org/10.1016/j.cortex.2016.03.021

Shanker, S. (2016). Self-Reg: How to Help Your Child (and You) Break the Stress Cycle and Successfully Engage with Life. Penguin Press.

Shilling, V., Morris, C., Thompson-Coon, J., Ukoumunne, O. B., Rogers, M., & Logan, S. (2013). Peer support for parents of children with chronic disabling conditions: A systematic review of quantitative and qualitative studies. Developmental Medicine & Child Neurology, 55(7), 602–609. https://doi.org/10.1111/dmcn.12091

Siegel, D. J., & Bryson, T. P. (2011). The Whole-Brain Child: 12 Revolutionary Strategies to Nurture Your Child's Developing Mind. Delacorte Press.

Siegel, D. J., & Hartzell, M. (2003). Parenting from the inside out: How a deeper self-understanding can help you raise children who thrive. Tarcher.

Siller, M., & Sigman, M. (2002). The behaviors of parents of children with autism predict the subsequent development of their children's communication. Journal of Autism and Developmental Disorders, 32(2), 77–89. https://doi.org/10.1023/a:1014884404276

Slade, A. (2005). Parental reflective functioning: An introduction. Attachment & Human Development, 7(3), 269–281. https://doi.org/10.1080/14616730500245906

Spagnola, M., & Fiese, B. H. (2007). Family routines and rituals: A context for development in the lives of young children. Infants & Young Children, 20(4), 284–299. https://doi.org/10.1097/01.IYC.0000290352.32170.5a

Steiner, A. M. (2011). A Strength-Based Approach to Parent Education for Children With Autism. Journal of Positive Behavior Interventions, 13(3), 178–190. https://doi.org/10.1177/1098300710384134

Stern, D. N. (1985). The Interpersonal World of the Infant: A View from Psychoanalysis and Developmental Psychology. Basic Books.

Sussman, F. (2012). More than words: A parent's guide to building interaction and language skills for children with autism spectrum disorder or social communication difficulties (2nd ed.). The Hanen Centre.

Swartz, J. R., Wiggins, J. L., Carrasco, M., Lord, C., & Monk, C. S. (2013). Amygdala habituation and prefrontal functional connectivity in youth with autism spectrum disorders. Journal of the American Academy of Child & Adolescent Psychiatry, 52(1), 84–93. https://doi.org/10.1016/j.jaac.2012.10.012

Ting, V., & Weiss, J. A. (2017). Emotion regulation and parent co-regulation in children with autism spectrum disorder. Journal of Autism and Developmental Disorders, 47(3), 680–689. https://doi.org/10.1007/s10803-016-3009-9

Torres, E. B., Vero, J., Drain, N., Rai, R., & Bermperidis, T. (2025). Hidden social and emotional competences in autism spectrum disorders captured through the digital lens. Frontiers in Psychiatry, 16, Article 1559202. https://doi.org/10.3389/fpsyt.2025.1559202

Tronick, E., & Gold, C. M. (2020). The power of discord: Why the ups and downs of relationships are the secret to building intimacy, resilience, and trust. Little, Brown Spark.

Tronick, E. Z., & Cohn, J. F. (1989). Infant-mother face-to-face interaction: Age and gender differences in coordination and the occurrence of miscoordination. Child Development, 60(1), 85–92. https://doi.org/10.2307/1131074

White, J., McGarry, S., Williams, P. J., & Black, M. H. (2025). 'We think differently, we learn differently, but at the end of the day we're not that different': Strengths-based approaches in high school from the perspectives of autistic adolescents. Autism, 29(11), 2804-2817. https://doi.org/10.1177/13623613251348557

Wilbarger, J. L., & Wilbarger, P. L. (2002). Wilbarger approach to treating sensory defensiveness and clinical application of the sensory diet. In A. C. Bundy, E. A. Murray, & S. Lane (Eds.), Sensory Integration: Theory and Practice (2nd ed., pp. 311-338). F.A. Davis.

Yan, T., Hou, Y., & Deng, Y. (2025). Parental Burnout in Chinese Parents of Children With Developmental Disabilities: A Generalized Additive Model Perspective. Journal of Autism and Developmental Disorders. Advance online publication. https://doi.org/10.1007/s10803-025-07151-w

Yuan, N., Weeks, H. M., Ball, R., Newman, M. W., Chang, Y. J., & Radesky, J. S. (2019). How much do parents actually use their smartphones? Pilot study comparing self-report to passive sensing. Pediatric Research, 86(4), 416-418. https://doi.org/10.1038/s41390-019-0452-2

Özbay, A., Karakaya, B., & Aşcı, S. (2025). Perfectionism as a mediator between obsessive-compulsive symptoms and overcontrolling parenting in autism spectrum disorder families. International Journal of Developmental Disabilities. https://doi.org/10.1080/20473869.2025.2578601

www.ingramcontent.com/pod-product-compliance
Lightning Source LLC
LaVergne TN
LVHW010916110826
845149LV00013B/2381

* 9 7 8 1 9 7 2 6 5 9 3 2 8 *